Codepen.

Relationships

A Step by Step Recovery Guide to Save
Relationships Affected by Codependency.
How to Stop Controlling People and Start
Living a Healthy Life to Be Codependent
No More

Robert Mayer

Codependent Relationships

Table of Contents

Codependent Relationships

INTRODUCTION

First off, I would like to thank you for purchasing *Codependent Relationships*. I sincerely hope that you are able to resolve your codependency and improve your life 100-fold. You may be looking at the word codependent and thinking, "That's a strange word." For the most part, when a word is preceded by "co," it typically describes something that has more than one component working together. Back in the '80s, this word likely made much more sense when used to describe the relationship of an addict and their partner. But times have changed.

If you were to walk through the park and ask the first-time people you saw what they thought the word codependent meant, you would probably get a lot of strange looks, but you would also get several different definitions. Codependent used a lot, but many people don't really understand what it means. Codependency has stuck around in the world of psychology. It isn't some fad. It has grown with the times and has moved into other territories other than addiction and has morphed into something that likely touches your life. Once you make it to the end of this book, you are going to have the real meaning of codependent. You will likely also start spotting coworkers, friends, family, and possibly significant others hidden within these pages. You might even see yourself.

Throughout this book, we are going to look at every type of form of codependency. You will soon realize that codependency lives within a person's mind and it can also make up their entire identity.

This book is here to help you learn all about codependent relationships so that you don't wind up becoming stuck in one. The following are just a few of the different ways that you will learn how to get out of a codependent relationship:

You will discover skills, such as journaling, that can help you through.

You can work with a partner to help you change.

You learn who you really are and you break your need for codependency.

You will spot patterns within you and others.

You will learn new ways to communicate to prevent codependency.

Through codependency quizzes, you will learn a lot more about yourself.

The goal of this book is to give you plenty of psychological insight into codependent relationships with a helping of personal growth mixed in. The majority of people who buy these types of books are looking to make their relationships better. If this is you, then congratulations, you are in the right place. You are going to get to see codependent relationships through another's eyes. This will help you to adjust your views so that you don't end up missing out on other important things.

You are going to learn how to embrace you and live for you. You will discover that you have value and that you don't need anybody or anything else to provide you with worth.

Codependent Relationships

CHAPTER 1

What Does Co-Dependent Mean?

Something that everybody can relate to wants to feel needed by somebody. A codependent person takes this too far. They put all of their time and energy into one-sided relationships where reciprocity has never lived.

The word codependent made its first appearance back in the 1930s. Since then, the term has begun to evolve through practice and usage to find different places in our culture and language. There are many psychiatric terms that have worked their way into our lexicon, like dysfunctional, narcissistic, and passive-aggressive, and like those words, the meaning of codependent has become muddied after moving from therapy use to the public. Through its 75 years of use, codependent has changed, so you really need to understand its usage throughout history to fully understand what it means.

Its First Appearance

The 1960s created a lot of change in the world, and psychology was no exception. There was a great upheaval in the established way of thinking. The psychological view of therapy for the mentally ill was changed in the way people were treated, issues were studied, and how they were identified. Before then, nobody ever even thought about involving the family within the treatment. Therapists typically would only see the person with the problem.

Codependency would never have been discovered if psychology theory hadn't been expanded upon to include the elements of family systems theory, the recovery movement, self-help movement, and assertiveness training. Through these changes, it provided the psychological world with new concepts and for the established concepts to grow. This helped to improve their understanding of the behavior of humans. Codependency became one of those concepts.

Codependency began as a single part of recovery literature. Nowadays, it has become more widely used in psychology, social work, and psychiatry. While therapists work to treat codependency within therapy, the DSM (*Diagnostic and Statistical Manual of Mental Disorder*), which is a mental health care book that helps professionals bill, diagnose, and treat disorders, doesn't have it listed.

Family Systems Theory

Codependent is used to help describe a set of dysfunctional patterns of behaviors, emotions, and beliefs that are caused by a person's interactions with their world, especially with their family interactions. Until the family system theorists started their study, nobody had ever thought to look at things other than the patient's mind to figure out their psychological problems. This is what makes this theory so important.

The two big figures within the family systems theory are Murray Bowen and Virginia Satir. During the '50s, they were able to break out of the established medical model and create a new way of looking at human actions. Bowen and Satir have been cited as part of the top ten most influential therapists.

Murray Bowen, MD

Murray Bowen, according to the Bowen Center, began his psychiatric training at the Menninger Foundations in Topeka, Kansas in 1946. Throughout his 40 years of work, Bowen established a different understanding of the way human behavior worked. He discovered that the actions of a person emerged through their interactions with their personal environment. The Bowen Theory change how therapists worked with their patients.

Virginia Satir

Virginia Satir has been lovingly dubbed as the "mother of family therapy." While she was a member of the Human Potential Movement, she and Bowen worked together. From the '50s through the '80s, she ran a parallel course with Bowen, but she was more hands-on with her approach to the systems theory in working with families. She didn't think that it was an issue to bring another person into therapy to help the patient. Satir discovered that a bigger problem existed and that the family system could help to treat it. Since she did so much work on the family system and all of the connections that family could create, it makes sense that discovered codependent interactions early on in her work.

In the article, "New Face of Codependency," it is stated that Satire studied more than 10,000 families and discovered that 96% of the families showed some type of codependent actions and thoughts.

Satir published her book, *Conjoint Family Therapy,* in 1964. She would end up publishing eight more books. The work that she did on a family theory created an important change to move from the illness model to a model that looked at personal growth and awareness.

The Big Change

To believe that a patient's psychological problems had a connection to their family was revolutionary. Satir found that no matter who is suffering, it is the conditions that exist to the family system that is going to make and maintain dysfunction. During this time, it was very much a startling idea. It would go on to change how psychiatry and psychology would progress in treating psychological problems.

Let's take a moment to really think about the family system.

Think of the family system as a mobile, like the ones you hang over a baby's crib. Let's assume that the mobile represents an anorexic ten and her entire family. Hanging in the middle is the girl and around her is her codependent mother, rebellious brother, absent father, and perfect older sister. Every single piece is connected and balanced in some way, but each piece shifts and moves. If you were to touch one of these people, you will start to see things change. When a therapist begins to work with the family, they poke at the mobile. Through the use of family therapy, the balance is going to shift, which will create a bigger space for change and healing and gives the family a chance to change and create balance. This gives a place for recovery.

Alcoholics Anonymous

AA may have worked outside of what was considered mainstream mental health, it was the first large scale group that identified codependency as a major problem in

alcoholism. During the '40s and '50s, the 12-step program of Alcoholics Anonymous showed up in the US and all around the world. During the early years, they focused mostly on the individual, almost as if they lived in a vacuum. This is the area that codependency was often used the most. It was used as a way to describe the alcoholic's spouse or significant other. It may be said that AA was able to influence the family systems theory, or possibly vice versa. No matter which way it worked, both were able to reach the same conclusion: The family plays a huge part in recovery.

During the early 1950s, the realization that alcoholism was a family problem showed up in recovery literature. Years later, Melody Beattie would write *Codependent No More*. This would become one of the first books that would give readers an in-depth explanation of codependency in an alcoholic family. She also wrote it in such a way that everybody could understand the idea. Her work illuminated and expanded upon the concepts of displaced anger.

Recovery Movement

By this point, we now have the distinct literature of AA and the family systems theory. While they were both written slightly differently, they shared the same message. They both validated the role of the family when it came to treat psychosocial ills, addressed how complicated the connection of family relationships was to keep a disease or empowering change and focused on interpersonal relationships.

What is now called the Recovery Movement didn't just include AA, but also all of the groups that shared the same beliefs of empowering others to recover with through group of peers. All of these groups have existed along with professional mental health services and provide aid to people who are struggling with divorce, parenting, grief, depressions, spending, eating disorders, abuse, gambling, and more.

While the 12-step program of AA began life as the first treatment for addicts, AA has also been able to encourage people to get their family involved with the treatment. AA has even expanded to create programs for adult children of alcoholics, codependents, teens, and spouses. This has moved us towards a family systems approach.

We now have a strong network of recovery groups that help people dealing with many types of mental health issues. Each one has its own unique focus, but they all follow a similar format to AA.

What Does This All Mean?

With codependency's history and the realization that family is a big part of mental health, let's take a look at what codependency means. Codependency tends to be a behavior that a person has learned from older generations. It is a behavioral and emotional condition that prevents a person from being able to create a healthy and mutually satisfying relationship. There are some people who refer to this as "relationship addiction" since a lot of codependents tend to form or keep a relationship with a person who is abusive, one-sided relationship, or emotionally devastating. Through many years of studying the way families of alcoholics worked, researchers discovered codependency and the fact that it is learned through watching and imitating people around them who display certain behaviors.

Codependency can affect siblings, friends, parents, co-workers, or spouses of a person who is dependent on alcohol or drugs. Originally, codependency was only used to refer to partners in chemical dependency, people living with, or dating an addict. But, through the years, they have found similar patterns in people who are in some type of relationship with chronically or mentally ill people. Today it is now used to define any codependent person from dysfunctional families.

A dysfunctional family is one where members suffer from fear, shame, anger, and pain that is denied or ignored. Some of the most common issues can include:

- Some form of physical, sexual, or emotional abuse.

- A family member who suffers from a mental or chronic physical illness.

- A family member who is addicted to drugs, gambling, alcohol, sex, relationships, food, or work.

Dysfunctional families aren't able to see that there is a problem. They aren't willing to confront or talk about the problem. This causes the family members to repress their feelings and ignore individual needs. This creates "survivors." They start coming up with actions that will allow them to ignore, avoid, or deny hard emotions.

They work hard to detach their self. They won't talk about, confront, feel, or trust anything. The development of identity and emotions of the family members are often inhibited.

All of their energy is focused on the family member who has the problem. The codependent person sacrifices their welfare, safety, and health for the others. This can end up causing them to lose contact with their sense of self, needs, and desires.

Codependents tend to have low self-esteem and will look for things outside of themselves to find some type of happiness. They don't know how to be their self. Some people will turn to drugs, nicotine, or alcohol, which then turns them into an addict. Others can become compulsive with other habits, like gambling, work, or sexual activity.

Codependent Actions

Every single codependent has good intentions. They work

hard to try and help others who are going through some type of difficulty, but their actions become defeating and compulsive. Codependents are often martyrs and benefactors to another's needs. A wife may try to cover up for her alcoholic husband. A mother may create excuses for their misbehaving child. A father may try to "fix things" for their child so that they never have to face the consequences for their actions.

The main problem with this is that rescue attempts provide power to the needy party to continue acting the way they always have and to become more dependent on the caretaker. As their reliance grows, the codependent begins to feel satisfied and rewarded for being needed. Once the caretaking turns compulsive, the codependent will start to feel helpless and like they don't a choice in their relationship, but they can't do anything to stop the actions that have caused this. Codependents feel that they are the victim and are attracted to this type of weakness within relationships.

They have a hard time seeing that they have a problem, but to the outsider, it is quite obvious. They believe all they are doing is helping a person in crisis. At first, the codependent person may have set out to try and help the person work through their problems. Over time, this was probably not reached. They adapt to this dysfunction and they focus on trying to maintain the status quo. The thoughts of ending the relationship create more pain than the thoughts of staying.

Codependency Growing

Codependent behaviors are often rooted in childhood. Children who had parents who were uncaring or abusive may set aside their own needs and be to follow self-sacrificing behaviors just to survive. If their parents suffered from a mental disease or addiction that wasn't treated, the child could end up becoming the caretaker. Children in these types of situations will sometimes be considered "parentified." Parentification is "the reversal of the parent-child role."

Since these children have been forced to grow up faster than they should have been, their own developmental needs haven't been met. There is a good chance that this could end up creating a cycle of codependency that is passed through the generations.

This can be particularly harmful when it comes to parents of addicted children. A parent who is codependent to an addicted child can enable the actions of their child, even when their goal is to help. The fact that parents of addicted children are at risk of becoming codependent, proves the concept of codependency has significantly grown since the original framework of what used to just be the relationship between spouses or children of addicts.

But these things don't have to come from home. Children who have been sexually abused may not be able to create their own sexual identity and satisfaction. This places them at a greater risk of placing the needs of sexually demanding partners before their own needs.

CHAPTER 2

Common Co-Dependent Relationships

While the lady who will give you the shirt off her back, the caregiver, and the peacemaker can all be codependent, this isn't always the case. There are codependents that are also angry, cranky, manipulative, and resentful. If you start thinking about the main problem that codependents rely on the views of those around them to let them know that they are doing okay, then it is easy to see the importance of another person's opinion. This places them in a powerless position.

When couples start counseling, the therapist has to spot the different dysfunctions in their relationship and help them to fix these problems. At various points, the therapist will take a look at the strategy to see how it is going. The therapist must be able to see the different changes happening to figure out what can help the relationship.

With the different case studies that we will look at, you will start to get a good idea of the various ways that codependency can appear in a person's life. Codependent people come from different walks of life, are of various ages, and lifestyles. You will also learn that codependency doesn't just exist in romantic relationships but can occur in every relationship.

John and Regina – The Alcoholic Brother

Regina has established herself as an elementary school teacher in the small town she lives in. Her brother, John, lives in New York and is an aspiring actor. Ever since they were teens, Regina would deny that John had a drinking problem. She would come up with excuses and has done so for years. If there was ever a time that he looked drunk on stage, she would just say that he was tired from working long hours. When he didn't come to family reunions, she would explain that he was too busy. When John got a divorce, she blamed his wife, saying that she had been cheating on him.

Whenever he called Regina for money, she would send it to him and hide it from her husband. One day John gets arrested for attacking somebody during a bender. Regina lets her husband know that John is sick and needs some help. She travels to New York to be with him. She has to even take money out of her retirement to get him out of jail. Once out of jail, John takes her credit cards and skips town. Regina's marriage just barely makes it through this after her husband finds out. Regina is codependent on her brother, John.

Rebecca and Mom – Aging Parent

Rebecca is the oldest child of ten. She grew up on the family farm in Wyoming. She is fit to become the third-generation cattleman and will inherit the farm will her parents pass away. It has been expanded to include crops as well. The entire family pulls their weight to take care of things. When she is 16, her father dies and her mother relies on her a lot to help take care of the farm. This has caused Rebecca to have to grow up quickly.

Unlike her, all of her siblings leave home once they graduate. Rebecca stays back, gets married, and continues to take care of the family business. Her mother helps out with her grandchildren and does as much as she can with gardening and cooking. Rebecca's husband works as well as helps with the farm. They make it through tough times when everybody works together.

Rebecca's mother suffers a stroke at 60. She and her husband have to tend to her mother until she recovers. A few years later, though, she suffers another stroke. This one leaves her paralyzed on one side. Rebecca's sister comes in to help out for a couple of weeks and some of the other siblings help with expenses and to take her to physical therapy.

The mother ends up falling and hitting her head, which causes you to lose her ability to talk and walk. As usual, Rebecca tells everybody that she will tend to her. As Rebecca's children head off to college, it becomes harder to care for mother and take care of the farm. Her husband has been helpful throughout this, but he thinks that her siblings should be helping more. Rebecca doesn't want to burden her siblings, and she says the mom won't do well with big changes.

Mother's health continues to deteriorate, and her husband begs her to reach out to her family. Rebecca won't do it. In a desperate act, her husband speaks to their local Commission on Aging. The therapist says that they should come together for a family meeting to figure out how everybody can help. Rebecca is upset when she finds out and decides not to participate. Her husband goes to the family session and six siblings show up. Since Rebecca doesn't want them to feel inconvenience, she grudgingly goes.

The meeting ends up helping. Her siblings say that they will try to help out. Several say that mom can live with them a few months at a time. Two say that they will help pay for her daily needs. One says that they will take her to her doctor's appointments. Rebecca leaves the meeting feeling relieved, and thanks to her husband for help.

But, the first time that her sister says that she can only keep mom for a couple of weeks, Rebecca tells her that it is okay. When her brother quits helping with the medical bills, Rebecca doesn't say anything. Since Rebecca is unable to hold them accountable, the whole system falls apart.

Rebecca established a codependent relationship very early on with her mother. From that point, this pattern of codependency continues through her entire family.

Bea and Alex – Helicopter Parenting

Bea is a single mom to a 15-year-old daughter, Alex. Bea often calls her daughter "her life." She feels bad that Alex only has one parent, and she tends to overcompensate by trying to make her happy. Whenever Alex looks upset, Bea does things for her or gives her things. She works full-time, but Bea always makes a point of volunteering at her daughter's school and has done so since she was in third grade. She was her daughter's troop leader until she dropped out. She volunteers for Alex's cheerleading squad and always drives them to away games. Bea loves it when her daughter talks to her about her relationships, good times, and bad times. She provides her daughter with advice and becomes upset if she doesn't follow it.

She sees Alex as the "perfect" daughter, but her grades have begun to fall. Bea panics and talks to Alex's teachers every week to discuss her grades. She gets her a tutor to try in get her math grade back up to an A. Bea has decided on her own to send out college applications and to ask for catalogs.

When Bea gets an appointment with Alex's principal to talk about Alex's breakup with her boyfriend, the principal calls her a "helicopter parent." This leaves Bea feeling angry and unappreciated.

The connection between Codependency and Narcissism

There is a tricky connection between narcissistic and codependent types. Codependents have very little in the way of a personal relationship with their self. Everybody else's needs are placed before their own. This isn't healthy at all.

Narcissists are another type that doesn't have a healthy relationship with their self. They put all of their importance ways over the importance of others. They use others to get what they want, and they exploit their relationships without feeling a bit of guilt or remorse. They blame others for their problems and they can't see that they are doing anything wrong.

With this piece of information, it is easy to see how these people find each other. They are two puzzle pieces that connect. One becomes the victim for the other, but the connection goes deeper.

A familial link has been discovered between these people. If a person has a parent who is narcissistic, they have an equal chance of becoming narcissistic or codependent. This remains true even if both parents are narcissistic.

As a codependent begins to recover, they will begin creating boundaries and will have to face the narcissist. Many people find it hard to conceive of a person who can't empathize and learn from previous mistakes. The main mistake that codependents make is giving a person the benefit of the doubt, especially if they have a narcissistic partner because they find it very hard to believe that a person could be that selfish. This creates a new cycle.

The best thing that a codependent can do is to learn that the narcissist doesn't understand what compassion is, which a big component of all human beings is. Since codependents tend to blame themselves for problems, they will often find great success with a therapist. This isn't the same for the narcissist. They are stuck in their own world of non-blame, which is not conducive for change. How is a person going to change if they don't know there is anything wrong?

CHAPTER 3

Are You Co-Dependent?

There are a lot of people who discover that they are in a never-ending cycle of unhealthy relationships, despite good intentions. In fact, the struggles I have had in my life with my relationships are part of the reason why I wrote this book.

As we now know, the traditional definition of codependent has to do with the maintenance, control, and nurturing of relationships with people who have a dependency on a chemical substance or engage in bad behaviors. The first model of this was an alcoholic husband and his spouse.

McGovern and Dupont (1991) believed that the codependent person shares responsibility for the other person's unhealthy actions, mainly because they keep their focus on the actions and create a connection between their wellbeing and how the other person acts. Le Poire (1992) believes that healthy people nurture the other person when they act on negative behaviors. This is great for the sick person, which only works to reinforce their problem. In Beattie's 1987 book, she says that the person in the relationship that has the most control is the powerful one and the other person becomes indebted.

There is an unspoken agreement between the people in this relationship. The person that is dependent might not be as passive or innocent as they come off. These questions and signs will help you to spot codependent relationships.

1. Do find yourself keeping quiet in order to keep from creating an argument? Codependent people want to feel as if they are making things easier for the other person. If an argument happens, then that means they haven't done their job.

2. Do you even feel as if you are trapped in your relationship or underappreciated? It takes a lot of energy to be codependent and take care of another person's life. This is all done under the guise of wanting to help. When a person rejects or ignores advice from the codependent, it causes the codependent to feel angry, unappreciated and abused.

3. Do you often worry about how people view you? The happiness of the codependent all depends on other people. If others show that they don't like them, then they won't like their self.

4. Do you often cover up the problems of your family members, friends, or partner? Since codependents

never deal with their feelings, they figure out ways in which to lie to themselves about how a person is their life is behaving. Since they feel responsible for the other person's actions, they will rationalize it or blame others, or blame themselves, in order to stay in control.

5. Do ever find that you have a hard time telling them no when they ask you for something? The codependent is afraid of rejection and failure. In their wrapped thought processes, they feel as if they are unlovable. Codependents find it very hard to trust others easily or to share with then openly because they are afraid that they will be exposed.

6. Do you ever find yourself making extreme sacrifices to make another person happy just so that you feel like you have a purpose? Codependents are always willing to go above and beyond in order to make others happy. They want to get approval, love or feel as if they are accepted and liked. If they are unable to get this approval, the codependent feels as if they are the victim.

7. Do you feel like you are responsible for fixing the problems of others? A codependent feels as if they have to solve other's problems. They think that the other person needs their help. They believe the other person

isn't able to make the best choices or choose the right course of action to fix their problems.

8. Do you find yourself giving advice to people whether they have asked for it or not? Codependents often jump at the chance to provide a person with advice. They are able to provide people with an endless stream of good advice about whether other people ask for their opinion or not.

9. Do you expect other people to do the things you say? When a codependent provides advice, they expect that advice to be followed. Codependents are unable to understand the concept of boundaries.

10. Do you often take this very personally? Since codependents don't have boundaries, any comment, remark, or action reflects back on them. This makes them feel like they have to be in control.

11. Do you ever feel like you are a victim? Everything that happens to the codependent or the other person reflects on the codependent. This leaves the person feeling powerless and victimized. They can't understand their role in creating their own reality.

12. Have you ever tried to use guilt, shame, or manipulation in order to control the actions of others? In order to get their way, codependents act in a way

that will force others to comply. This can be unconscious or conscious. Since the way a person reacts is a reflection on the codependent, it's extremely important that the codependent feels as if they are in complete control.

It is really not that surprising when a codependent turns to addictive behaviors in order to help them work through their unresolved feelings. They turn to things like alcohol, drugs, or food to help control their emotions or they will choose to take part in actions that are considered risky. When this starts to happen, they can easily end up losing control. This will cause their addiction and codependency to worsen. Their mental and physical wellbeing is impossible to reach. The only way to fix this is to go through rehab.

CHAPTER 4

The Personality of a Co-Dependent

Codependents have an innate ability to attract other people into their life who aren't motivated or interested in participating in a give and take relationship. By constantly choosing narcissists or addicts as romantic partners or friends, codependents tend to find their feeling disrespected, undervalued, and unfulfilled. While they likely complain and they feel resentful about the inequality of their relationships, codependents feel as if they are stuck and can't change.

The passive codependent will often be fearful and avoidant when it comes to conflicts. They will try to influence or control their partners through carefully executed strategies, and most of them will go unnoticed. This is because they have a fear of being alone, low self-esteem, and tendency to find themselves in relationships with people who are controlling, abusive, or dangerous. Since they make sure that they are hidden and secretive in their controlling actions, they tend to be viewed as the more manipulative codependent.

Then the active codependent tends to be more bold and overt with their manipulation tactics. They aren't as afraid of harm and conflict, and they have a bigger chance of starting arguments with their partner. These people are sometimes viewed as slightly narcissistic since they are open with their actions. While they are constantly in a cycle of trying to control others, who aren't interested in meeting their needs, they still don't feel any urge to end the relationship. They believe fully that they can "fix" the other person. This never happens.

While both of these codependents may look different on the outside, they both have an "others" self-orientation. They will often stick close to addicts or narcissists while also experiencing feelings of unhappiness, resentfulness, and anger because the relationship lacks reciprocity. While active codependents will sometimes appear to be stronger, both have very strong insecurities. Neither one of them can break free from their relationships.

Codependency is not only booking into two subcategories of active and passive; those can also be broken down into five other subcategories.

Martyr

For this codependent, suffering is a virtue, especially when it comes to placing the needs of others before their own. At least these are things that some people will learn from the family, religious institution, or cultural heritage. At work, this type of codependent will pick up extra projects and is normally the last person to leave at night, choosing to say no to drinks with friends. If they do go out, they will always pay without being asked, even if they don't really have the money.

When a person's being is completely made up of sacrifices, it will often cause them to neglect their needs for love and care. Ironically, this is the same reason these codependents are trying to get the appreciation of others. This tends to backfire. Not only do they tend to resent those that they help, but the other person will either take everything they do for granted or will resent the codependent as well. Martyrs tend to be a type of active codependency.

Savior

The world is a scary place, but the savior is here to protect everybody. When their child is facing some type of problem at school, they are in the principal's office the next morning to fix the problem. When their friend can't make rent, again, they will give them some cash, again, so that they don't end up being kicked out.

Everybody is going to need help at some point. But when there is a person that feels personally responsible for providing other people will comfort, they strip that person of their chance to take care of their own comfort and wellbeing. The codependent will enable that person's self-limiting actions and will send them messages that they are helpless. With time, the other person may start to believe this. This is a type of passive codependence.

Adviser

To get a good idea of this type of codependent, take a moment to think about the *Peanuts* comic strip. Lucy is the perfect example. She sits from daylight to dark at a makeshift desk providing others with advice about anything and everything. This person could have a great skill in helping people through their problems and offering them some clear options. They too believe that they have great insight into the problems of others. Listening, though, may not even be the strength of theirs.

This is definitely a tango type of situation. This codependent tends to see people who seek advice as a person who doesn't have a lot of self-esteem. But the things are, the people who feel as if they have to control and advice others have just as much insecurity. This is what is called borrowed functioning. The codependent takes charge and tells others what they should do, and they are just as needy as the other person. They need to have a person let allow them to be in charge to help give their self-esteem a boost. They are both dependent. This is a form of active codependence.

People Pleaser

This codependent will be the one volunteering at their children's school and helping all of their neighbors fix things. They are the ones that volunteer to make the coffee run. They love it when they get to feel the love and bask in all of the praise for their generosity. But there is darkness to all of this.

The codependent reaches the dark side when they start to no longer feel appreciated, or when the thoughts of doing something feels like a chore. They know they have reached it when they start to use their skills to control people. They have the belief that other people will like them for all of their favors instead of liking them for who they are. This is a type of passive codependence.

Yes Man

This is the person who says yes to everything even if they really want to say no, and they end up resenting them. They will fake a smile in agreement with others instead of telling the truth. They will always remain passive with their romantic problems and they won't tell them when they get upset.

Therapists will often hear comments like, "We never fight," from people in therapy. They will look at their therapist for some type of approval, but all this lets them know is that there isn't any honesty within the relationship. Not having any conflict within a relationship isn't a good thing. Look at it from a business perspective. In a business where most people are "fine" with their jobs and they don't complain tend to do so because they are afraid of losing their job. When you push away your real feelings, instead of trying to find a good way of sharing them, will create problems. This is a type of passive codependence.

Building Codependency in Childhood

It may be hard to think of a child as a codependent. As humans, we begin to form psychosocial problems from the moment that we are born. Children respond to people and things that happen around them from the get-go. Children are just starting to develop their personality traits up until they reach their teenage years, so it might be better to say that early programming could end up in causing codependency traits later in life.

Let's take a look at this example.

Susan is the good little helper. She is six and has turned into "mama's little helper." She likes it when she gets to help her mother with cooking, cleaning, and taking care of her younger sibling who is 18 months. Her mom and dad always thank her for all of her help. She basks in the praise, especially when her mother tells her friends how much she appreciates Susan. "I wouldn't be able to do this without her help," mom says. Susan is sometimes given the opportunity to serve the drinks to the members of her mom's card club. Susan will then sit to the side, quietly, as they play their cards.

Susan's dad is busy. Every day when he gets home, Susan removes his shoes and props his feet up to help him relax. She takes him his paper and gets him a beer. He gives her a kiss on the cheek and smiles. "That's my good girl," dad says as he relaxes back and starts to read his paper.

There are a lot of signs that signal the development of caretaking behavior. Girls at the age of six should be out playing with their friends. A child should be self-centered. This is how they learn to develop their sense of self. Of course, it is a good thing for children to spend time with their family, but this time is best spent playing games, talking about school, reading, and the like. This is an unbalanced dynamic. Susan is taking care of her parents when they should be the ones taking care of her.

Fortunately, Susan begins to outgrow this, but as she does and begins to pull away from her parents and wants to spend time with people her age, her mom begins pouting and saying things like, "Who is going to help me with the baby?" This is when Susan reaches the second phase of programming. Her parents don't reward her for being a typical child. Instead, they make her feel guilty if she doesn't take their needs into consideration. When she takes care of their needs, she gets thanked, which creates codependency. Susan is slowly being trained to believe that other people's needs are more important.

As she becomes a teen, Susan will become more worried about what others think of her. She turns into the teacher's pet and starts people-pleasing and makes sure that her mother's needs come first. Susan is going to end up being a caretaker and feeling as if she is the one responsible for others and will ignore her own needs.

Adolescents

A person will reach their fifth stage of development when they reach adolescence. This is normally between the ages of 12 and 18. This is the time when they focus on Identity VS Role Confusion. Teens tend to struggle with fitting in and they try to figure out who they are. They create close ties, figure out how they should interact in intimate ways, and they think about their morals. This is the weird between phases of not being a child yet not being an adult.

Here's an example of adolescent forming codependency.

Sabrina is 15 and a sophomore in high school. She reached puberty before most of her friends. By 13, she has already fully developed. All of sudden, she not looks older than all of the other girls her age, which causes her to receive a lot more attention from boys, and even men. At first, she finds this as terrifying. On the inside, she still feels like a child and is completely confused by this attention.

While a child, Sabrina was taught that she had to get approval and attention from adults. She had to become the "pleaser." All of her worth was dependent on taking care of other people's needs. It started with her parents and then it grew into helping her teachers and other adults.

With the new body that she has developed, she had found that there are new ways to make people happy, sex. Sabrina doesn't find the boys in her class interesting. She wants to fit in with all of the popular girls, but they don't like her. Boys, on the other hand, love to be around her. Anytime they ask for something, she wants to help them out. Through different sexual encounters, Sabrina believes that she has discovered approval. Only after does she end up feeling guilty.

Unfortunately, her need to gain people's approval has also caused the other students to judge her. Now the popular people definitely won't accept her. She has reached an identity crisis. Despite trying to get people to like her, she sees other people viewing her as bad and unlovable, and these are all things that she wants to avoid.

Sabrina never developed an internal compass and her external judgments have caused problems. She is in a place that could destroy her self-esteem. She feels completely hopeless and tries to commit suicide, which puts her in the hospital.

She is still alive, so that is going, and that means there is hope.

With some help before her personality solidifies, she could end up going through the rest of her life without being codependent.

This is going to be a rough road for Sabrina, but with the right help, she will learn where she made the wrong turn. Insights will help her to discover who she truly is.

Parents

Codependency is most often passed down in the family. If unhealthy patterns continue to live in unconsciousness, it won't be changed. If you aren't aware of something, how can you change it? As you move through this awareness, it's important that you don't start to feel guilty and beat yourself up when you begin to realize that you may have modeled codependent behavior for your children.

What parents want is for their children to grown up in a safe environment so that they can be healthy functioning adults. Parenting is amazing, but it is also daunting. A perfect parent does not exist and that is okay.

Here's another example.

Duane and Amy got married right out of high school. They bought a house and had a couple of children. Amy's life revolved around Duane. They uprooted their family and moved across the country for his job, which meant she lost touch with her family and friends. She thought they were living the "American dream," by Duane though otherwise. With his next promotion, he left his family.

Amy was left with no job and two children to care for. She became depressed from being abandoned. She found a job in a store, but it didn't enough to take care of her children. The savings she had received from the divorce didn't go very far. She had to sell the house and move them into an apartment. As a single parent, working six days a week for minimum wage, Amy was very happy with the way her life was turning out.

After two years, Amy decided she needed a new husband. She had to find somebody that could share the burden and help her care for her kids. She would get a young girl down the hall to babysit whenever Amy wanted to get drinks before coming home. It didn't take long before she started to meet men.

What was originally just a short-term plan of finding a new husband quickly became a lifestyle for her? She found out that she loved the single life, dating, and being taken to fancy restaurants. It was as if she were living two lives. She doesn't tell her dates about her children. Since she is still in her 20s, she fits in with everybody else. The issue with this is, she isn't really like everybody else because she is a mother.

Then she meets Jack, and he seems to be the perfect guy, but, on their first date, he says he doesn't like kids. Amy thinks that if he falls in love with her, he will like her kids, so she stays in the relationship. For a year, the children barely see their mom. She is up early to get to work and then the babysitter comes over after school and three days a week, the babysitter puts them to bed. Amy travels a lot with Jack on the weekends. She leaves right after work on Friday and doesn't get home until Sunday night after the children have gone to bed. On the weekends, an older lady in their building keeps the kids.

The children first have to face being abandoned by their father, and now their mother is abandoning them. Every single day they are faced with uncertainty. They sometimes get to talk to their mom on the phone, and they constantly beg her to not go out, but she tells them that she has to go on another adventure. What she tells them and what she shows them are different.

Amy's codependency in her marriage with Duane prevented from connecting with him in a healthy way. She was always worried about being exactly what he wanted her to be. This pattern continues into her manipulative dating habits. Amy wants to find a person so that she can become who they want her to be. Her relationship with Jack is getting ready to reach its boiling point. She won't be able to pretend she doesn't have kid forever. Amy has hidden from Jack for months now. He is going to eventually find out, and then he is going to start questioning what kind of woman she is. The horrible part is the way that he affects her children.

Friendship

Actions of codependency are most often seen within the most intimate relationship. This can create subtle codependent actions, or it can create rippling patterns. Codependency can be occasional or chronic.

Let's look at Tonya.

She has a friend, Rhianna, who she hasn't seen since they graduated high school. Rhianna e-mailed Tonya letting her knows that she had just gotten a divorce as was moving to Buffalo where Tonya lives. Tonya has been there for 20 years now. Rhianna lets her know that she is afraid of moving there, so Tonya tells her that she will help her get settled in and sets up a lunch date.

Tonya is already at the restaurant when Rhianna rushes in. They hug, sit, and Rhianna immediately starts complaining about all the traffic. She hates all the crowds and asks Tonya why she didn't suggest a place that was closer to her house.

As the waiter comes up, Tonya smiles and greets him nicely. She frequents the restaurant and knows him. When he brings them their order, Rhianna is upset? She says the portions aren't big enough. The waiter asks if she would like more soup or bread, but the nicer he tries to be, the angrier Rhianna gets. Eventually, she tells him to take the salad away and asks for a burger. She eats the burgers, but fusses that it was "undercooked." For the rest of the two-hour lunch, Tonya has to listen to Rhianna rant about her ex.

Rhianna starts calling Tonya up every day to ask her for recommendations. When they meet up, Rhianna complains about the suggestions Tonya made. She is angry that Tonya's dentist caused her gums to bleed. Tonya leaves this lunch feeling tense.

Tonya is throwing her annual holiday party and invites Rhianna. After the party, Rhianna starts complaining about how the guests were rude to her. Tonya listens for a bit and then excuses herself. Tonya begins screening calls, so she doesn't have to talk to Rhianna. Tonya's husband resents the negativity that Rhianna has caused for them.

Tonya understands this, but whenever she sees Rhianna, she feels she has to spend time with her. She starts hiding the lunches she has with Rhianna from her husband.

Tonya doesn't know how to create boundaries with Rhianna. She doesn't live Rhianna all that much at this point, but she feels stuck. Tonya constantly feels stressed, and at home, she jumps every time the phone rings. She knows the things her husband says are true, so now Rhianna is affecting her marriage. Tonya hides things from her husband. The problem is, Rhianna thrives on anger and Tonya is codependent on her and doesn't know how to end the relationship.

Codependent Relationships

CHAPTER 5

What Are They Thinking?

Codependency revolves around fear. It creates actions that are formed from feelings of anxiety and creates hyper-vigilance in relationships. This is how it breaks down in the brain: when a person feels scared the left brain, which controls language, stops working. Remember back in school when you knew the answer but couldn't figure it out when you were put on the spot? The part of the brain the remains active, no matter how afraid a person feels, is the emotional section, the right side. People still have the ability to scan their environment and read the emotions of others even when they are terrified. This part of the brain works overtime when a person is scared.

An extremely scary moment for a codependent is when they realize a relationship isn't working out. Having to face the dissolution of a relationship is tough for anybody, and it is only natural that people try to figure out how to keep it going. But, for a codependent, they do things to their own detriment to keep the relationship going.

This causes them to feel bitter, exhausted, resentful, angry, and lonely. This can turn them into martyrs and they start to complain about the things that they have done without getting anything in return. There are many times when they do go to extremes.

Once the relationship does come to its natural end, they are filled will grief and guilt, and they could be stuck obsessing over what they could have done differently. Some may even try to beg their way back into the relationship. This is their attempt to try to get things to work in their favor.

Some of the most common things that codependents do to try and keep a relationship from ending are:

- Fall into depression

- Turn inconsolable

- Threaten their ex

- Tried to figure out something they could do differently

- Refused to speak up for what they want

- Try to be seductive

- Beg or plead

- Remain financially dependent so that they are unable to leave

- Try to make them feel guilty

Admitting these things is very humbling, but it is an important part of recovering. Being honest with yourself is hard, but it is a good idea to look at your past behaviors in order to help yourself change. I myself have done a few of those things.

At a very young age, I was taught that my actions in public would either embarrass my parents or make them proud of me. Complying with my family's religious beliefs could either save face for my family or ruins them. I didn't know what was happening, but I build a subconscious belief that I had power over them. If I made sure that I did everything correctly, then everybody was happy.

Codependents also have a fear of abandonment, or they have experienced neglect or abuse in their life. When the fear of abandonment starts to appear in a relationship, they start trying to do whatever they can to keep things the same.

Codependent Triggers

The triggers that codependents react to are different for everybody and depend on their personality and history. Triggers could be considered wounds that were created from past trauma. When triggered, the codependent starts living through their past trauma.

There are even internal triggers. A person can trigger their self into feeling shameful if they aren't able to reach their own standards. The inner critic has the power of ruining your entire day. Codependents thing they have to self-sacrifice, so when asked for help, it may trigger them. Another trigger for codependents is being told that they are being sensitive or selfish.

Then triggers can be external. An external trigger can cause an overreaction and these happen when the intensity and duration of their actions are higher than normal. Overreactions often happen when triggers remind them of somebody from their past. It's hard to spot these triggers because, in the eyes of the codependent, their perceptions are normal. Experiencing an overreaction can create the experience that the codependent didn't want in the first place.

Some of the most common triggers include:

- Seeing a person in trouble

- Being asked for help

- Someone becomes angry

- Being put on the spot

- Being criticized or compared to another person

With your new understanding of codependency, we are now going to move into looking at what you can do to overcome your codependency and improve your quality of life.

CHAPTER 6

Getting Help

You have to start the change if you are going to recover from codependency. You aren't the reason the person is addicted, so you can't fix it. You can't control the actions of others. It is fine to help other people, it is a nice thing to do, but you have to put yourself first. It isn't possible for you to be there for other people when you can't be there for yourself. The first thing you need to do is a thorough self-examination.

Recovery isn't going to be easy. You are going to have to make a complete reversal of your patterns so that you can connect with yourself. Once you begin to heal, you will experience:

- The capability of being truly intimate

- Autonomy

- Congruent values, actions, thoughts, and feelings

- Authenticity

This change will require four steps:

1. Abstinence: This is the biggest part of your recovery. The goal is to focus on you. You need an internal locus of control. This means your motivations should be based completely on your values, your feelings, your needs. You learn how you can meet those needs in a healthy way. You don't have to be perfect at this step- in order to see progress. Perfection is also impossible. So far, you have depended on others and give into them. Instead of abstinence, you have learned how to detach, please others, and obsess over them. With abstinence, you will learn autonomy and become self-directed. If you have been subjected to an abusive person or an addict, you may worry that you will upset your partner. This is will require a lot of courage to break these patterns of conceding power.

2. Awareness: Denial is the biggest problem with addiction. This is true for the person addicted to drugs as well as the person who loves them. Codependents not only deny that they are "addicted," but they deny their needs and feelings, especially when it comes to nurturing and intimacy. Codependents may have faced a childhood without being nurtured, their emotional needs never being met, and their opinions and feelings weren't respected. Over time, they end up learning how to ignore their needs and believe their needs are wrong. People will try to either be self-sufficient or they find

comfort in negative ways through sex, drugs, food, or work. This creates low self-esteem. To undo this, you must become aware of what is happening. Negative self-talk is the biggest killer of self-esteem. Most people aren't even aware of this internal voice that pushes them and criticizes them.

3. Acceptance: Self-acceptance is a big part of recovery. This is something you will have to focus on for the rest of your life. A lot of people turn to therapists for help without realizing that most of the work revolves around accepting themselves. Ironically, before the change can happen, you need to accept your situation. You will learn a lot about yourself during recovery that you will need to accept, and life is going to present you with many limitations and losses. This is what is called maturity. When you accept your reality, you will find possibilities. Change is then able to happen. You will find the energy you never knew you had. Feelings of guilt or loneliness can turn into compassion and action.

Self-acceptance teaches you that you don't have to make everybody happy. You will learn the best way to take care of your needs and you will learn to forgive yourself as well as others. You will be able to be self-reflective without beating yourself up. You will get to see your self-esteem and confidence grow. You won't let other people take advantage of you. You will learn to be authentic and assertive.

4. Action: Insight can only take you so far. Eventually, you are going to have to take action. You are going to have to take some risks and move out of your comfort zone. This could mean speaking up for you, doing something you have always wanted to, going places along, or setting boundaries. You will need internal boundaries to commit to yourself and external boundaries where you say "no." Instead of feeling like you have to use others to make you happy, you will learn how to take care of your needs yourself. Each risk or new behavior you try, you are going to learn something new. You will create a sense of self. You will find positive feedback when this happens.

Words are actions as well. The things you say reflect on how you feel about yourself. Learning assertiveness takes time, but it is one of the most powerful recovery tools. Being assertive means, you know yourself. It means you have limits. It means you honor and respects yourself. You write your own life.

With this in mind, let's go over some things that can help with your recovery. These things are only the first few steps that you need to take. There are plenty of other things that you can do, and they will be covered later on in the book.

What Are My Strengths?

When your life has been spent helping other people, you have probably lost touch with you. You have likely lost your identity within the problems of other people.

Right now, you need to take some time to reflect on what your talents, values, and strengths are. More importantly, once you have identified those things, you need to live your life by positively using them. This is going to reestablish your life so that you can have your own identity.

What Things Make Me Happy?

The person you have been trying to "help" is likely too focused on their own problems to help you meet your needs. Being codependent causes you to neglect your needs in order to help somebody else.

You have to stop letting yourself be neglected. Take some time to think about your own needs and desires and what you should be doing to make sure that you are truly happy.

What Are My Finances Like?

Whether you want to admit it or not, you have probably helped others with their finances to some degree or other. While you might not be buying those drugs or alcohol, but if you are helping them pay their bills, groceries, or legal fees, it all equals out to the same thing. They use their money for their habits and you use your money their needs.

All of this could leave you in a sticky financial situation. This creates more worry and stress. Now is the time to take a look at your finances and make sure that your obligations are taken care of before anything else. This will release a lot of worry and stress. When your bills are paid, your needs are met. You won't feel anxiety or resentment when it comes time to pay them. This will also force the other person to face their own financial problems.

How Do I Interact with Others?

As your codependency was growing, you might have noticed that you withdrew from people. Feelings of shame and guilt have prevented you from asking people for help. Eventually, you noticed that you felt isolated, and the other person had become your entire world.

However, during recovery, you will learn how to use your time and yourself in healthy ways. You will learn new ways to interact in healthy ways with people, especially with those people who had begun to ignore.

What Shouldn't I Do?

While a lot of these may look like they appeal to codependents of addicts, they still apply to anybody who is a codependent because codependents act in similar ways.

1. Don't let yourself be overwhelmed with shame and guilt. If you do have to deal with an addict, there are

more than 24 million Americans who are struggling with addictions, so you are not alone. Almost everybody knows somebody is addicted to something. This is the same if you are codependent on an aging parent or your child.

2. Don't nag. Everything that you want to say to them, they have probably heard a million times. They could have even said it to their self. If you harp on the same things, they will quit listening.

3. Don't preach. Acting "holier than thou" just pushes people away.

4. Don't try to "fix" them. This is very true when you are dealing with an addict. The sooner you start to realize that addiction is a disease that has a treatment, the better it is going to be for both of you. You can't fix them.

5. Don't try to control them. No amount of arguments, threats, or convincing is going to make them act how you want them to.

6. Don't feel responsible for what they do. You aren't the one making them do anything, they are. They control their life as you control yours.

7. Don't stay with an abusive person. 20% of people who are abusive are also addicted to drugs and 70% are alcoholics. Over 90% of abusers have admitted that they had used drugs or alcohol the day that they attacked their significant other.

CHAPTER 7

Making Personal Changes

Everyone won't choose to go see a therapist for help with their codependency problems. This book isn't advocating a one and done approach either. No matter how you choose to work through your codependency, the exercises in this chapter will help. They can also help when they are used with therapy or in group therapy.

Journaling

You may have had a diary when you were younger. It might have been a small book with a fancy cover that had a small lock and key. When you got older, you may have written in a journal about your deepest, darkest thoughts, gossiped about friends, and cried over heartbreaks.

Now while you are starting to explore your codependency, it might be helpful to start journaling again. You can do it however it suits your needs. You can use your computer; a spiral bound notebook, three-ring binder with paper, or an expensive leather journal.

A Vault

Your journal can become a vault where you keep track of the work you have been doing on your codependency. It is a place where you can come back to when you need to remember the way you felt or thought about something or to give yourself a pat on the back for the journey you are on. Journaling is used in many self-help groups or during therapy because they have been proven to work. When you are journaling, you don't have to wait for your next therapy session or call a friend. You don't have to work around family obligations. Find a quiet place, get your journal, and write down all those thoughts and feeling that seem important when they happen.

There are many people who are afraid to put their feeling and thoughts on paper. They are afraid that somebody might find their journal and read it. Adults who were abused during their childhood might have anxiety about being discovered, their secrets, and their privacy. Everyone needs a private place to keep their personal things. You might want to keep your journal locked in your car. While you work through your problems, you may feel more confident with some privacy.

While you are thinking about using a journal, you may want to try some of the ideas you find in this chapter. You have the choice to write in a planned, organized way, or unstructured, free-flow style.

Using Mindfulness

This term has become very mainstream in the past few years. This term describes a way to focus on what you are experiencing at any moment in your life without judging it. There is a lot of evidence that mindfulness is a wonderful tool that can help you manage and prevent addiction relapse and physical illnesses. It could help improve your quality of life, reduce stress, anxiety, and depression. Mindfulness is similar to meditation, yoga, and other practices that have roots in Buddhism and Eastern religions. The great effects that these practices offer have been firmly established from years of research. In order to show how accepting mindfulness has become, schools are introducing mindfulness as a part of their daily routine.

Having a state of mindfulness is important when working with your codependency. It could take you away from all the distractions in your life. It can help you understand yourself intimately, get rid of any negative talk that goes through your head, and accept yourself for who you are. This practice could improve your overall happiness. It may create a place where your new insights and creativity could emerge and flourish. With the help of your journal, mindfulness could help you observe yourself and how you are at each moment. It could help your codependency by pushing you away from blaming yourself and old judgments. You may want to start each session with a mindfulness exercise.

Using Mindfulness with Meditation

Mindfulness doesn't have to be formal. It also doesn't need to take a whole lot of time. Techniques like noticing your breathing, sitting quietly, and allow thoughts to enter your mind without evaluating them as either good or bad and can happen in just a few minutes. Once you become familiar with the way this works, you can get into this state when you feel you need to for as long or short a time as you would like.

The following is a simple meditation:

Have a seat on the floor. You may sit on a folded blanket or pillow. Sit in a crisscross applesauce position just like a child would. Just make sure you are comfortable. Make sure your hips are higher than your knees. Put your hands on your thighs with your palms up. Place your index finger and thumb together. Keep your spine straight but don't be stiff. Use your spine's natural curve. Keep your shoulders back slightly with your chin forward. Keep your eyes focused and open. Focus on the floor about six feet in front of you. Some people will have something to use as a focal point. If you decide to do this, keep the same distance of six feet.

Breathe east and begin noticing your breath. Don't focus too closely on it. Just breathe and let it happen. Place your attention on the environment and body. Just notice it. This meditation doesn't want to clear your mind. Thoughts are important to mindfulness. Notice these thoughts running through your mind like a ticker tape. See them, but don't make judgments. If you become too involved with your thoughts, you will begin to lose awareness. Gently bring yourself back and focus once again on your breathing. If your state to breathe too fast, notice it, and return it to a relaxed breath. The main goal is to be mindful of whatever is happening. There isn't any wrong or right here, just breathing.

You can practice this meditation for ten minutes. You can start to lengthen your meditation time to 30 minutes or more over time. The amount of time you want to devote to your meditation is totally up to you and it won't be wasted. When this gets too easy, you can do this anywhere you would like.

Anger: Silence the Storm

Healthy anger is just a tiny cloud that moves over the sun. You are the only person who can turn anger into a storm. Once you add your provoking talk to this angry cloud, you might stir up a huge storm. Before you know it, you are Dorothy. You are swept up and you swirl out of control. You aren't even certain about where you will land. You could easily unwind if you can learn to change the thoughts that helped make this anger. You are able to calm yourself if you feel anger starting to stir. You could do this with journaling and mindfulness.

Codependency and Anger

As stated above, there is healthy anger. Anger might be a signal of a boundary violation. If someone comes up to you and hits you, it is reasonable to raise your voice. It is also understandable that you insist this person stop kicking you. Unreasonable anger is what causes you to stop enjoying life and causes you to destroy your relationships.

People who are codependent usually have resentment, anger, or rage problems because they are constantly looking for disapproval. They may become honed into their partner who has become their ego mirror. They brace themselves for rejections, constantly on edge wondering if they are okay. If they are confronted with an image that isn't perfect, they may get angry and start bullying a person into being silent or make them change their mind. At times, anger will fuel comments that try to punish their ego mirror for their bad impression.

Once you can accept the fact that anger is made by you, you will be well on your way to recovery. It doesn't matter if anger is outwardly expressed or simmers deep inside you in the form of resentment, it is going to affect your peace and keep you away from people that you care for love. Rage is extremely destructive to anybody around you and yourself. It is extremely important for you to master your rage. Just like any feeling, anger is based on intensity. It can run from mild irritation, frustration, and possibly into a full-blown rage.

People who are codependent are normally angry because they are constantly trying to control everyone else. This is something that won't ever be achieved.

Look Out for Gathering Clouds

A good way you can use the body-mind connection when trying to rescue anger is to do regular exercise like walking, running, and swimming. These activities might help you identify a "zone" of well-being. Making physical activity a part of your daily life can reset a trigger for anger.

It would be like walking on sharp rocks. This can make your body tentative and tense and makes you brace for injuries. The least little thing will set you off when you are in this state. When endorphins kick in and you have a relaxed mind, you feel like you have entered a beautiful meadow that makes you feel comfortable, trusting, and relaxed while you are walking. The occasional tickle of grass gets enjoyed instead of felt.

Another way to achieve inner peace is by practicing Zen techniques like guided imagery, massage, mindfulness, tai chi, relaxation techniques, breathing, meditation, and breathing. If you can learn how to do some of these techniques each day, you could change your anger threshold. You could write about your Zen experiences while you journal.

Mindfulness could help on the front lines, as well. Body sensation will give you your first clues to your anger rising.

Your heart rate is going to increase, your breathing will get shallow, your jaw is going to clinch, your muscles will tighten, your voice might rise, the tendons in your neck will start to stand out, and your eyes might narrow or widen. Write any of these signals down in your journal. When you notice a warning, you need to take a break and practice some sort of mindfulness technique until you are calm again.

It may be helpful to get some help from a significant another friend when working on your anger. Your significant other will help you a lot since they already see changes in your and they can sense your anger before you can. Your partner will change their position from being an enemy to be a friend. Choose a time when you normally don't feel angry. Agree to do an intervention where your significant other will tell you if they see you are getting angry. Remember that you asked them to do this, so you can't get defensive about what they might say to you. You have to agree to stop right then and there without question and take a break to do some mindfulness techniques. When you are calmer and are able to use the right communication skills, go back and resolve the problem.

Don't Seed Clouds

This is what makes your journal so helpful. Start by listing out everything that you are mad about right now. Look at the list and see if you have been trying to control a situation or a person that you can't actually control. Erase those things.

Look at what remains. Are there any you have some control over that would require some positive action? Erase them. Of the rest, which ones could you take action on, but you have chosen not to? Erase them.

Of the things that remain on your list, ask yourself what kind of motivation you have for action. Are you going to take some action to fix this problem? Is it going to improve a relationship? You need to make sure that your heart is in the right place instead of simply trying to be dominant over others. If you truly want to help, make an action plan. This will likely remove your anger list. Let go of everything you have erased. There is nothing that you can do about it. You are the one that is suffering because of your anger. Forgive and let go; it is the best thing you can do.

Getting the upper hand on your anger won't be as simple as erasing some words on paper. You have formed this anger habit over your life. You may have even accepted your anger as just a part of you, but it isn't. You might have justified your actions by thinking that you have to act badly because you are angry, this isn't healthy. Since codependents see their self as the victim, they act self-righteous when they express rage.

When you start to notice you feel angry, or you get angry, don't seed the clouds. Practice the different journaling techniques in this chapter to work through it. Write down a list and give yourself the chance to solve the problems without becoming angry. This will be ongoing, at least until you have gotten control of your anger.

What Makes You Angry?

This is a great exercise to do. You will be writing provoking self-talk down in your journal. All these entries are going to show you exactly how you make yourself angry. In just a couple of sentences, write down the incident that made you upset. Then, draw a line down the middle of the page. On the left side of the page, you will list the self-talk that creates more anger. Then, on the right side, write down a statement that could lessen your anger.

Here's an example of how this could work.

Johnny is upset with Darla because she overdrew their checking account. They have had this argument several times in their relationship. He would often get angry, accusatory, and self-righteous whenever he saw the account was overdrawn. Let's look at how Johnny could use this exercise to work out the problem. He draws out the two columns and in the first column he starts writing down his anger causing self-talk:

- She purposefully does this to upset me.

- She is selfish.

- She doesn't care about me.

- I work hard for the money, but all she does is spend it.

- She won't listen.

On the right he writes down what could lessen his anger:

- Our money management isn't working, what can we do to fix it?

- We are partners, is there anything I could do?

- She could use some help.

- She works as well, and I spend money as well.

- She is busy.

This will provide you with more information about yourself. A lot of people think other people "make them angry." Can you see how this plays right into codependency? Blame is externally motivated. To change these patterns of codependency, you need to find internal motivation. You need to understand why you do what you do, why you feel the way you feel, and then use this information for inspired action.

Finding the New You

You could use the same techniques to help you be the person you were before you developed feelings of hurt, anger, and resentment. Start to notice the things that you do in life. Do you keep a frown on your face? Are you tense? Look in the mirror. How do you look? Happy or discontented?

If you take a moment to think back to your childhood, to a time where you were cranky, your mom might have said that your face would freeze that way. You know, now, that this isn't true, but the body will hold onto memories. If you are outside on a sunny day, listening to upbeat music, walking around and enjoying nature, and your face looks upset, then you have probably been wearing that look for most of your life. This life of a codependent means traits of being everything at all times, overworking, inflexibility, high standards, being disappointed, trying to please others, and self-doubt. This can all be exhausting and frustrating and will affect your wellbeing.

With your journal, start writing down time where you felt loved, warm, peaceful, tender, excited, safe, and content. You must remind yourself that you can love. Try to do this as often as you can.

Choose a place that is quiet where you won't be interrupted. Pick out a happy moment that you have written about. Close your eyes for a moment and try to recreate this moment. Maybe it was when you held your baby for the first time. Really remember the moment; the color of the blanket, the people in the room, how the baby looked and smelled their little hands and feet. Allow yourself to feel all this joy. Then, notice how your face, breathing, and muscles have changed.

If you and your significant another fight a lot, think about a time where you felt close to them. Allow all the bad feelings slip away and release the resentment and bad things that you have held onto. Really allow yourself to get into this. Once you have done this, write down everything that you love about your partner. When you start to feel distant, meditate for a moment before you try talking to them.

If you really want to change the way you feel, try to do these exercises every day. The worst part of being codependent is being disconnected with yourself. Whatever you are able to do to help you stay connected will change the way you view yourself and it will, with time, empower you.

CHAPTER 8

Ending Your Co-Dependent Relationships

If you draw several rings and place a person in the center, every ring that expands from the center to the outer edges is people that have influenced them. The ring that is closest to the middle is the people who have the strongest influence on them like their partner or children. This will make them care about how their family feels, the way their family behaves, and what their family thinks. Someone who is codependent relies extremely heavily on the way their partner influences them. They don't just care about what their family feels, thinks, or does. They need their family to define who they are. Their partner turns into their ego mirror. They become a person with whom they can count on the show them their value and self-esteem. The bad news is this mirror doesn't have grey areas; it will reflect in either completely black or white. This means they see themselves as either damaged or perfect.

Ego Mirror

This term gets used to describe either one person or several people who get used by a codependent person to substitute the way they look at themselves. People who have well-formed, intact identities don't have a need for an ego mirror. They know themselves inside out. They don't identify with how they are reflected for somebody else. They listen to people whose opinion they value and when they care for. Anybody else won't be able to rock their foundation by disagreeing with them, judging them, or having conflicting needs.

If you think back to your childhood, you probably remember the story of "Snow White," the evil queen continuously goes to her mirror and asks if she is still "fairest of them all." The codependent person's partner is that mirror. Just like this evil queen, a codependent person has to be constantly reassured that they are superior. They can't even handle being told the truth. They need their mirror to tell them that they are the best. If they are ever told they aren't the best, they will fly into a rage and will try to destroy whatever caused their misery. They will basically "smash" their mirror.

A codependent person's identity could be shattered easily because it is so brittle. This is why they are desperate to change all negative feelings no matter the cost. They don't know how to change themselves inwardly, so they have to change on the outside. If push comes to shove, and if it means breaking the mirror, they won't hesitate to break it. Until it gets to that point, they will use any weapon they have at their disposal to force people to get rid of all concerns that might show that they aren't perfect.

Codependent people don't have the freedom to let other people be who they truly are. They can't stand to see others angry with them. They can't stand for anybody to think badly of them or be disappointed with them. They are tied to a certain reflection forever. They are in a place of pain since the only way for them to feel good about themselves is to make sure the mirror reflects them well.

Let's see how you answer these questions:

- Do you get panicky if you think your partner is mad at you and you don't know why?

- Are you constantly desperate that your partner knows your point?

- Do you give in to your partner's needs and then feel resentful?

- Can you handle it if your partner gets mad at you? Do you ever try to change how they feel?

- Do you feel uncomfortable if your partner asks for your opinion without telling you theirs?

- If you are having a deep discussion do you try to figure out how your partner feels before you ever share your feelings?

- Do you ever take your partner's advice and think it over without getting defensive?

- If you have expressed opinions that aren't the same, is there a way you can agree to disagree with them?

- Are you always aware of your partner's moods?

- Do you begin to get anxious if your partner walks away or ends a discussion before the conflict is resolved?

- If your partner criticizes you, is there a way you can listen without explaining yourself in different ways?

If you said yes to at least one of these questions, get out your journal and write about it. Think about a time that you reacted this way to your partner. Figure out if you can find a way to talk them out of how they feel, why you have to have their approval or are always trying to convince them of your position. If you need your partner approve of each action, though, and feeling, you may be using them as your ego mirror.

Ego Mirrors, Guilt, and Codependency

A person who is a narcissist and a person who is codependent will be lacking the same things at their core. Neither one has a healthy identity of themselves. Beneath the narcissist's bravado is a person who needs everybody else to validate their ego. Their ego mirror needs to show that "the world revolves around me," "better than thou," and a puffed-up sense of themselves. If they see any faults, inadequacies, or imperfections, the mirror is horribly wrong.

Narcissists won't feel guilty because they don't have any conflicts with their identity. They are perfectly okay with the idealized self. They just need their ego mirror to make sure they are shining pure white all the time. If the mirror doesn't give this to them, they try to find a new one. A narcissist's reflection looks like a perfect diamond to them at all times but unfortunately, it is just a big piece of glass.

For a person who is codependent, their identity always looks like a gem with flaws. It has blemishes, cracks, and its color will be off just a little bit. This isn't saying that they are undesirable, they just aren't perfect. Each diamond is just as shiny as all the other diamonds, but a codependent person knows there are flaws. They have conflicts since they know the flaws are always there. They just can't accept their flaws. They need that ego mirror to show them their brilliance instead of their flaws.

A quote from Elizabeth Kubler-Ross sums it up perfectly: "People are like a stained-glass window. They sparkle and shine when the sun is out, but when darkness sets in their true beauty are revealed only if there is light from within."

A person who has positive self-esteem and healthy ego will accept their imperfections along with other people's imperfections. A person who is codependent can't. They won't ever accept their flaws and work extremely hard to deny them. They have to see themselves as shiny and possessing wonderful qualities at all times. They try to be selfless, helpful, considerate, loving, and thoughtful. If they ever realize that they aren't, they start feeling guilty. If they happen to see their flaws in their ego mirror, they will never be able to accept it, even though they know it is true. Instead of looking deep inside themselves, they just attack the mirror.

Misdirected Guilt

You know that codependent people have an unrealistic sense of self. Their behavior may not match up to their distorted self-image. If this were to happen, they always blame the ego mirror.

Wes and Shirley have been with each other for over 22 years. Shirley is turning 50 and has been diagnosed with multiple sclerosis. Shirley's doctor meets with them and talks about the changes they can expect to happen with this disease. He takes a lot of time with them trying to help them learn how this illness is going to change their lives.

Shirley has always worked hard and is now going to have to limit her activities in order to keep her healthy. The doctor has asked Wes to make sure Shirley doesn't overdo it. He asks them to sit down and adjust their chores to help with Shirley's illness. Wes assures the doctor that he totally supports and understands Shirley. He is more than willing and happy to take on extra chores.

It takes them about a week to finally sit down and talk about what they are going to do. Wes agrees to do all the chores while Shirley will do more sedentary work like dealing with phone calls, paying the bills, and cooking. If any of their friends ask how Shirley is doing, Wes always makes a point of telling them that he is doing ALL the chores. He is making sure that she isn't doing too much and he is taking good care of her.

The truth is, Wes stopped doing any of the chores in just a few weeks. From that point on, he only did things after Shirley begged him to and then he wasn't happy about doing it. Shirley is having a hard time accepting her limitations and it is hard for her to ask for help. In only a few months and after the house begins to look like a pig sty, Shirley can't take it anymore and tells Wes they need to talk about the house.

Shirley: "Honey, I am feeling unnerved about how the house is looking."

Wes: "What do you mean?"

Shirley: "It is filthy."

Wes: "Oh, for God's sake, Shirley, it is fine."

Shirley: "No, it isn't. The toilets are permanently stained, there is burned on grease on the stove that won't come off, and there is something this smells up the refrigerator. There are cobwebs in every corner of the house and dust is covering everything."

Wes: "You are such a neat freak. You can ask any of our friends and they will tell you that you have OCD. Nobody expects a house to be as clean as you think it should be."

Shirley: "You think my standards are unreasonable?"

Wes: "Yep."

Shirley: "You promised me that you would keep the house just like it was before."

Wes: "Don't you think that is a bit ridiculous?"

Shirley: "No. That is how we have lived for over 20 years. Our house has always been clean and tidy."

Wes: "And you don't think it is that way now?"

Shirley: "No."

Wes: "Nobody in the world can ever please you, Shirley. You are way too fussy."

Shirley: "It completely bothers me to see the house this dirty and you keep telling me no to do anything, but you are following through on our agreement."

Wes: "Why do you always have to be so mean? You should listen to yourself. I wish I had a recording to play back to you of the way you talk to me."

Shirley: "Fine, never mind."

Wes: "That's right. Clam up like you always do. Why do you always get to end the discussion? You are mean. I'm going upstairs."

Wes' identity of himself is one where he needs to meet all of Shirley's needs and it isn't a realistic one. Wes doesn't want to admit that he isn't perfect. He likes making agreements that are based on his idealized self. He tells everybody that he is Superman, and there is that tiny part that truly believes him. When his ego mirror, Shirley, doesn't show him as perfect, then he attacks her. This has been going on for over 22 years. Shirley has learned ways to avoid conflict. If she just does all the chores, doesn't complain, then there won't be any problems and Wes can go on believing that he is perfect.

Let's say that Wes has been journaling to stop his

codependency. After he storms out, he takes some time to experiment with a mindfulness exercise. By doing this, he sees his behavior and doesn't make any harsh judgments. Because Shirley's self-esteem isn't at stake, he asks himself what he needs to do differently. Is there any way he can stop being so defensive and allow Shirley to feel the way she feels? How could he respond as a partner who is in a relationship that is interdependent? He knows he dropped the ball with the chores, and he does feel guilty. Wes made Shirley admit that she messed up instead of Wes messing up. Wes gets mad at Shirley instead of acting like a partner who truly cares. Shirley is Wes' ego mirror. Wes attacks Shirley and walked out. Is this the type of partner that he truly wants to be? Wes writes in his journal about this and goes back downstairs to talk with Shirley.

Wes: "Home, I am truly sorry about the house. You are absolutely right. I know I've said there isn't anything I wouldn't do for you, but I have dropped the ball on the chores. I know you too well to know that this upsets you a lot."

Shirley starts to cry: "I should have said something sooner before the house got so bad. I expect too much because it is hard for me because I am so weak now."

Wes: "I want you to know you aren't expecting too much, but I might not be able to keep my end of the agreement in a way that will make you happy. What if I pay for somebody to come in a few times a week to clean? I promise to pick up all the dirty clothes and do the laundry. I just can't seem to find the time to do everything else."

Shirley: "That sounds great. Maybe we could even find some time to go to the beach?"

Wes: "I would love that."

Stop Looking in the Mirror

This journaling exercise is going to help you turn away from your ego mirror. Your goal is to allow your ego mirror to quit their job. Let them be themselves, have their own feelings, reactions, and beliefs. It is going to be painful for this person to do time because they are a prisoner of your codependency. They can't be honest. They constantly walk on eggshells just waiting for you to have another meltdown or blow up. There isn't any way they can be rein when they are around you. Due to this, you tow can't have a relationship that is based on interdependency.

Write in your journal every day about your feelings and thoughts. Draw a line down the center of the page. Write down your codependent self-talk. Now you will counter that with interdependent self-talk. You have to know what the deepest problem you have to fix it. Because you are working on your identity, it is going to be worth all the work.

Make an account each day of your codependent feelings and

thoughts. Then you have to counter with interdependent thoughts. Here is an example:

- **Codependent**

  - Why in the world did he get so mad? Yes, I forgot to put the power bill in the mailbox. I didn't do it on purpose. He is just too rigid. He is a jerk.

  - She is overreacting. Why does she get upset about every little thing?

  - How could they be that mean? I worked for hours on that dinner and he didn't say anything about it. He will eat beans from now on.

  - They are never satisfied with anything. I fold the laundry wrong. I bathe the children and did it wrong. I have had it with their criticism.

- **Interdependent**

  - I said I would mail the payment for the power bill and I forgot. I'm not perfect but I do need to apologize and find ways to learn how to be more responsible. I would love for him to be able to count on me. Maybe I could begin writing things down.

- o She was extremely upset. I should have helped with the dishes. I should step up and stop being so blind to everything.

- o I can tell he is enjoying the dinner, but I need to hear it. I'll just ask him if he likes the chicken.

- o They have a problem with being a perfectionist. I like how I do things. Being a good dad and partner is up to me and I am very proud of myself.

It is fundamental to work on this part of codependency. The main goal is to know yourself and stop letting others define who you are. Use emotions to explore yourself. Big deal, your partner got angry just because you didn't do something the way they like it done or they do it. It got done and that is all that matters. This doesn't mean you did something wrong. Even if you did it wrong, this doesn't make you bad. Let your partner feel the way they need to. Acknowledge their feelings and move on. You are still fine.

Set Boundaries

You know there is a difference in how codependents think they should be and the real them with all their flaws. Due to this, a codependent person isn't always going, to be honest. They might make promises that are unrealistic because they think they should and not because they want to. They don't think it is fine for them to ever say no.

With time, deep codependency could become an unending cycle. You may hear things like:

- "If I were a better neighbor, I would help."

- "If I were a good husband, I would spend my weekends fixing the house."

- "If I were a good son, I would ask my parents to move in with me,"

- "If I were a good dad, I would get a loan to pay for my child's tuition."

It isn't possible to be everything to everyone all the time. Because of this, a codependent will let people down and this, in turn, makes others angry. To their horror, they are then seen badly and this reinforces their poor self-esteem.

Being Assertive

One way to help you set boundaries is to practice being assertive. You will do this first in your journal and then in person. You can take the time to write about whether you feel assertive when you have to deal with your partner. Assertiveness will be describing ways to set boundaries or being able to tell people "NO" in a way that won't be aggressive or argumentative. It shouldn't be tentative or vague. It is a way to deliver your message that is direct, firm, and kind.

Do you have any of these illogical beliefs?

- My partner will leave me if I let them down.

- If somebody needs something, I must give it to them.

- I can't bear the thoughts of hurting anyone's feelings.

- My needs aren't as important as other people's.

- If I'm not generous, people aren't going to like me.

- If I don't help, people will think I am selfish.

- I am being unreasonable if I don't do this or that.

While you are working on being assertive, use your journal to write down instances where you have agreed to do something that you actually didn't want to do and you resented it later. Put down what was going through your mind when you made the agreement. Try to get rid of all the "should" that are controlling your decisions. Figure out what created this need to please. Was it guilt or fear? Figure out what you were feeling, doing or thinking that caused you to agree to something and then regret it later.

For each incident, you can remember, figure out an assertive way you might have set a boundary. Write down as many responses as you can for each situation.

There may be a time when you were caught off guard by a request. Be sure that you have different assertive statements you can easily remember and use when needed.

You can use some of these examples to start your list:

- Son: "Could you bring me my notebook? I forgot it in my room."

  Mom: "I'm sorry. I hope you can do without it. I don't have time to bring it. I am completely covered with work today." (You don't need to get angry, whine about it, or blame him about how inconsiderate he is being.)

- Husband: "My mom called and I invited her for dinner tonight."

  Wife: "I would love for your mom to come to dinner. It just can't be tonight. I'm not feeling well."

- Wife: "Can you stop and pick up some wine for dinner on your way home?"

  Husband: "Sorry, not tonight. I am too exhausted."

- Daughter: "I need the car tomorrow for school."

  Dad: "Bad timing, dear. It is my turn to do the carpool at work."

Now think about some intimate situations where you may

need to set some boundaries with your partner that might be hard to do.

- Wife: "You have been on my mind all day. The kids are at the movies with friends. We are all alone."

  Husband kisses her: "That is such a great turn on, honey. Is it possible to get a rain check? I am exhausted tonight."

- Wife: "Do I talk too much?"

  Husband: "Sometimes, but I still love you." (He gives her a hug and kiss.)

- Girl: "Will you come to my house to meet my parents on Saturday?"

  Boy: "I am not ready to meet your parents, maybe sometime soon."

These examples above might seem easy, but actually, they aren't. The people who are closest to you expect you to always say "yes." They won't understand this new you, and they will feel unpleasantly surprised. You might want to let your older children and your significant other know what you are doing. You have been working on improving yourself. After they have experienced it, they will understand more.

Once you begin working on telling people "no" when you feel

like you need to, just remember the main factor is if you feel you might feel resentful later. If it might, saying "yes" is going to make you dishonest and it might have negative impacts on your relationship eventually.

It won't be long before you begin to understand your true self while working on your codependency. If you can learn to be honest with yourself, your responses will be more honest, too. While you are learning all this, if you realize you have agreed to do something and then see that you really don't want to do it, you can go back for a "redo." You can use the above examples and imagine you have said yes, but you want to change your mind. Here are some examples:

- Wife: "Will you run to the store for some apples?"

  Husband: "Sure, what kind?"

  Husband comes back ten minutes later: "Honey, I know I said I would pick up some apples, but would it be okay if I finished watching the game first?"

- Daughter: "Mom, can you trim my hair today?"

  Mom: "Sure, I have some errands to run first."

  Mom comes back an hour later: "Donna, I know I said I could trim your hair today, but I just don't have time. Can we do it tomorrow morning?"

How to Respond When Someone Tells You No

There are always two sides to each coin when dealing with codependency. There will have problems setting boundaries. If a person sets a boundary on them, they can easily get hurt or angry. They are equally critical of themselves and others. They expect a lot from others because they expect just as much from themselves. Because they don't have an identity that is solid, codependents react quickly to what they view as judgment. They see themselves as victims when other people mistreat them and feel disappointed or let down most of the time. It's hard for a person who is codependent to see others as being separate from them, especially their ego mirror. They don't think others need to have their own thoughts, behaviors, or feelings. Codependents tend to make everything about them. They will react quickly when they think somebody is being critical.

All the traits you can now see in yourself and the way you interact with your ego mirror can change with some effort. Use the strategies you have learned with this book and find a therapist if you think you need to.

CHAPTER 9

Improving Your Co-Dependent Life

The hardest but most fundamental responsibility that you will take on is facing your codependency and that of the people you are closest to. You will be taking a huge leap of faith, so you can become vulnerable with hopes of being a person who is more confident in the future. In order for this transformation to happen, you have to learn how to walk through your world with confidence and grace, set boundaries that are right for you, interact with people in a kind but direct manner, and be assertive when dealing with problems.

Learn to be a Better Family Member

Once you have learned your codependency patterns go back to your family, you may have discovered there are some skeletons in your closet. If you have been denying any shortcomings or abuse within your family, this might have been a rather painful revelation. You need to explore your family's origins, so you can understand your codependency.

Remember that you aren't perfect and this means that your family isn't perfect either.

Origins of Family

You have to use your journal and really think about your family. Try to write down any patterns or behaviors that might have caused you to become codependent. Make a heading for all your family members and try answering all the following questions:

- What feelings do you feel the most when you are around this person?

- Was this person around when you needed them?

- From what you know now, are they really codependent?

- From what you know now, are they really narcissistic?

- Were the chronically physically or mentally ill?

- Did this person express their feeling easily?

- Did they yell or blow up at you when they got angry?

- Did they make you feel loved?

- Has this person broken any laws or engaged in dangerous or reckless activities?

- Were they ever physically, emotionally, or sexually abusive?

- Did this person push any mistaken beliefs onto you?

- How did they deal with anger or handle conflicts?

- Did this person ever get addicted to drugs, smoking, spending, alcohol, gambling, anger, etc.?

- Did the person ever model any codependent behaviors to you? If so, what were they?

Once you have written about all your family members and answered these questions, see if you can find out or affirm what you know about your family and how they may have unknowingly planted the seeds of your codependency.

Now, take some time to look at what you have discovered and see if there are unresolved issued within your family. It doesn't help to dig up pain and hurt and leave it unattended.

Find out if you can resolve these problems by yourself, or if you need to address them with a certain family member. Your goal is to stop being a victim. What could you do to stop these ghosts from haunting you?

There are some ways you can look at all the information you found out about your family. One way is to find out how these things might be affecting your relationships now, how they could change your behavior with them. The second way is to find out if you need to confront the problems you have with specific family members. Will this help lessen their power over you?

Some people like working with just their current family meaning their significant other and children. Some people want to talk to their family members and parents that they were around while growing up.

Skeletons

Connie remembered that she had been abused by her older sister while she was growing up during the time, she was writing in her journal being mindful and reading. Her sister would constantly jump out and scare her. Patricia would lock Connie in her bedroom, steal her things, choke her, turn out the lights, break her toys, beat her up, and try to smother her with a pillow. Connie constantly told other people that she had a good childhood except for some "sibling rivalry."

Once Connie decided to take a close look at her childhood, she experienced all the pain again. She realized that it was necessary to look at this relationship she had with Patricia. She also begins to wonder about her parents. Where were they during all this abuse? Why didn't they try to protect her? Why didn't Connie tell her parents, try to stop the abuse, or do anything? Connie decided to see a therapist to get help for her depression and anxiety that was triggered by all these memories.

During therapy, Connie realized that she really doesn't trust anyone. Since she can't really trust her husband, it makes her controlling suspicious. This causes many accusations and arguments that get very explosive. She also realized that she still feels like a victim most of the time. She is constantly on edge just waiting for somebody to hurt her. Connie decided to talk to her husband about this and asked for his help with her childhood abuse triggers. Connie was able to work on her trust problems with her husband's help. This, in turn, actually helped their relationship.

Connie hadn't been in touch with Patricia for a very long time and doesn't expect to see her again. She doesn't want to confront her about all the abuse. She decided to write Patricia a letter in her journal. She won't ever send it to her. While going to therapy, her sister gets sick and asks Connie to come for a visit. Connie panics. She talks about these thoughts and feelings with her therapist.

Quick Tip: You can give yourself messages that are called positive affirmations. These are small statements that you believe are true. You can tell yourself things like: "I'm a survivor." "I am good enough." "I've got this." "I am strong." "I am not perfect, but that is fine." The main reason behind these affirmations and saying them out loud is to continue saying them until you begin to believe them.

Connie decided it was time to speak with her parents and tell them everything she had experienced while growing up. She told them that she was scared every day of her life. She asked them why they hadn't ever stepped in and stopped the abuse. Her parents were genuinely shocked by this news. They apologized profusely and asked if there was anything, they could do now to help her. Connie decided to forgive them. This alliance with her parents made Connie feel better about meeting with her sister. Connie doesn't feel as if she is a victim to all of them. She feels affirmed because her parents understand and will help her be nice to Patricia.

Connie chose to deal with the origin of her problems where she felt the most pain. She devoted a lot of time in therapy working through her childhood abuse and this helped her talk to her parents. She felt like she has resolved the problems she had with her parents and decided she isn't going to confront Patricia.

There won't ever be a right or wrong decision when talking about family origin wounds. If they are still abusing you, you might need to decide to tell them to stop. You can stop spending time with them and put firm boundaries in place. You may decide to deal with any unwanted behaviors when they come up. It is totally up to you.

Being a Better Friend

Once you begin changing and moving toward a life without

codependency, you will attract new friends. These friendships will be more interdependent and mutual. While working toward being an equal friend you are going to have two different aspects of friendship you will need to write about in your journal.

Getting to Know Your Friends Better

Just like you wrote about your family in your journal, you need to do the same thing with your friends. Don't worry about acquaintances, just the people you consider to be a real friend. Write their names at the top of the page. If you only have a few friends who are really close, this is totally normal. You could include friends that you think of as your second-tier friends. Now, you need to decide if your old friends still fit in with the new you. If these friendships are codependent, you can decide to move on, or you might decide to work on moving the friendship into a better place.

Answer these questions to help you figure it out:

- If you aren't available when your friend wants you, do they get mad?

- Are your friends very demanding?

- Do your friends ever cancel lunch dates or they just don't show up?

- Do your friends always ask for your advice?

- When you talk to your friend, do they talk more than 50 percent of the time?

- Is your friend unstable or fragile?

- Do you have to constantly walk on eggshells when you are around them?

- Are your friends not interested in what you are going through and don't realize you are struggling?

- Do your friends call and expect you to stop whatever you are doing and talk to them right then?

You may realize that some friends are making your life better. You are the only person who truly knows if the friendship is hopeless and you need to move on. If you decide to try to help them, these friendships might be helpful in giving you opportunities to consistently work on your codependency. Let's see what Paul did with his friends:

Paul Looks at His Friends

Paul has three close friends. Ed is his roommate; they work at the same place and see each other every day, but they don't have deep discussions. They ride to work together and their involvement is based on the apartment they share. Paul looks and his friendship with Ed and realized it is interdependent and they don't need to work on it.

Paul has another friend who is another work colleague. Aaron works in a different department than Paul but they are compatible. They have worked together on many projects and have had great results. They eat lunch together often. They normally talk about their hobbies, work, and video games. Aaron talks a bit more than Paul, but he likes to get Paul's opinion about things. If Paul were more withdrawn, he might be more of a listener and find himself in the role of a therapist. Aaron enjoys talking with Paul. Their relationship is an equal one.

According to his journal entries, Paul's third friend is the problem. Anthony also works at the same place but is needy and depends on Paul to help him on his projects. Lately, he has been asking for favors that don't have anything to do with work. Anthony is single, and Paul is drawn to him because Anthony needs Paul to help him. At first, Paul was pleased that Anthony asked him and enjoys Anthony's reliance and gratitude. Helping Anthony makes Paul feel good about him. Once Paul has worked on his codependency, he realized that Anthony's friendship isn't healthy. Paul has set boundaries telling Anthony that he is willing to help out at work, but he doesn't have time to help him after hours.

Fixing Problems

Look at your friends closely by writing in your journal. Are there any unresolved problems that you have been too afraid to talk about with them? Make a list for all your friends and process everyone. You have to decide if you can get rid of the problems you can't control you just don't want to deal with them. If problems are still there, try to approach them. If you learn to be more honest and forthright with your friends and they get offensive, you now to have information that could help you make better decisions about your friendship.

Before you start talking with your friends, you have to know what you want to achieve. What motivates you? If you are motivated to strengthen the friendship and resolve things by being honest, go ahead. If you feel brave enough to let them know they are being a jerk, just save your breath and let them go.

Look at Your New Friends

While you are changing, new people are going to come into your life. They will see you are compassionate, well-adjusted, and assertive; a person who is honest about how they feel and know their expectations and boundaries. This might not be what they are looking for. They may want to fulfill some codependency needs. They may want a friend who is codependent and will take care of them.

You now know enough about codependency to see red flags in relationships and friendships. Take care of any concerns you might have immediately. Remember to put yourself and your needs first and you have the right to stop any friendship that doesn't feel healthy at any time. If a new friend begins to cancel all the get-togethers you have planned at the start of the friendship, this might show that they aren't really interested in you at all. If your new friends begin to ask you for favors, this might show they are extremely needy. If new friends begin to talk about themselves nonstop, this isn't good either. If a new friend is offended easily, gossips about other friends get moody, misunderstands you all the time, these are all big red flags.

There is an old saying that goes something like: "Partners come and go but friends are forever."

Yes, friends are important for our emotional well-being, and some friendships do last a lifetime. Just make sure you pick your friends wisely.

Becoming Free from Codependency

Every person you meet in your lifetime and all the situations you face will give you an opportunity to fine-tune your freedom from being codependent. How can this change happen and what can you do to help it? Each year research finds something new about human behavior. Psychiatrists used to think that personality disorders can't be changed. Now, they believe just the opposite. The things that people believe can influence their behavior. At first, it was thought to be a brain thing. This it turned into an environmental/brain thing. Now, because of the advances in neurotechnology, research is newly excited about the brain. Many think neuropsychology will constantly evolve.

These changes that you have been trying to reach are very possible for you to achieve. Your goal is to develop and nourish your identity. Yes, you have an identity. Everybody does. You are only trying to remold your identity. Codependency traits are constant. You might be more or less codependent. You may show one or 50 codependency traits.

You have been given new insights, awareness, and tools that can help you fix your self-esteem, increase your sense of self, and be more confident. You will consistently be working on transforming by watching your behaviors, feelings, and thoughts. You make any adjustment you need to as you go along. You need to be present in your relationships and love. You have to value yourself. You have to find your voice. You have to learn to love yourself with all your flaws. You just might find that you have all sorts of power to expand your happiness.

CHAPTER 10

Getting Rid of Co-Dependent Communication

If you were to record a fight between yourself and your significant other, you may just realize that codependency has reared its ugly head during the argument. You have to create a vocabulary and some communication skills that will move you out of codependency to interdependency. This is like learning how to speak any new language. You didn't learn these skills during school, and you probably didn't learn anything from family or friends. You have to take responsibility for how you communicate. You must build a bridge that leads away from your true self while pursuing true connections with other people.

You Need to Focus on "I"

A critical part of learning to communicate well is learning how to use "I" messages. This tool is used when training Unites States diplomats. It was created about 50 years ago by our government. You can find this message outlined on the United

States Department of State's website. Now, the "I" message is a skill that is also taught during the couple's therapy. You will learn how to use this tool, too.

Shifting Internally

When you use an "I" message, it will restructure how you think and it will make you self-reflect before you speak. Since language shapes our reality, every time you use "I" instead of "YOU" when you try to resolve conflicts, you change your internal reality. This will force you to identify and process how you feel and how you perceive things before your mouth opens to speak about the problem. Just take a minute to think about how easy and automatic it is to start an argument with "You constantly do..." What does this language show you? You are seeing yourself as a victim. You want the other person to be at fault and you expect an apology.

Shifting Externally

During the couple's therapy, your therapist will begin communication training by introducing the "I" message. It will focus on the external or basically, what an "I" message is and ways you can use it to begin a conversation and help resolve conflicts. This is just part of the behavioral intervention. Most of the time, it is better to start changing your behavior and work toward an emotional and cognitive shift that will easily follow.

When you start a couple's therapy, the main purpose behind it is for you and your partner to change. You are the only person who is responsible for changing you. Your significant other is responsible for changing themselves. Most couples will begin therapy willing to start firing at their partner. To be ready for each session, take some time to think about how you can contribute to any problem you might have in your relationship.

How many times have you begun a discussion with "You need to," "You never," or "You always?" Every time you use "you" statement, you are blaming your partner for all the things you experience. You are painting a picture that you are a victim, and you are making your significant other defend or explain them. It is hard to imagine beginning a discussion by using "I", but it could have a huge influence on how the conversation is going to proceed. It can and will work. It is as challenging and as simple as that. You just have to change the word "you" for the word "I" when you start a sentence and watch the change happen.

The "I" Formula

The "I" message has three components: how you are feeling, what has caused you to feel like this, and the reasons behind why you have these feeling. It will look something like this: "I feel (a feeling, not thoughts) when you (a nonjudgmental description of behavior) because (a reason why you are feeling how you feel)." If you were to fill in the blanks, it might look a bit like this: "I feel threatened when you scream at me to turn off the radio because music helps me relax."

Here are some examples of "I" messages that you can use when you are trying to resolve conflicts:

- "I feel sad when you won't talk to me because my parents wouldn't talk to me when I was younger and this made me feel so alone."

- "I feel rejected when you laugh and make fun of me because my mom always made fun of me and it hurt."

- "I feel frustrated when your answer is defensive because this makes me think we can't talk to each other anymore and we are growing farther apart."

- "I feel angry when you tell me I'm lazy because I'm not; I do things my way and in my time."

- "I feel hopeless when you have promised me time and again that you will stop drinking and I see empty liquor bottles in the trash because this makes me think you are either an alcoholic or becoming one and you won't admit it and you won't get any better."

These examples show that when you can give an "I" message it makes you examine your feelings and the reasons behind them. It makes you share these with your partner without blaming them. Look at this statement and compare it with the previous one to see if you can see why it isn't a good "I" statement. Watch how it continues to get corrected until it fits into the right formula.

1. "I feel that you aren't listening to me because you are watching that stupid car show because you are a selfish jerk and this is all you ever care about."

2. "I feel unimportant* because you are watching that stupid car show because you are a selfish jerk and this is all you ever care about."

3. "I feel unimportant* because you won't look at me when I talk* because you are a selfish jerk and cars are all you ever think about."

4. "I feel unimportant because you won't look at me when I talk because I need direct eye contact, so I can feel like you are listening to me."

When you are trying to resolve conflicts, using the pronoun "I" show you are willing to share yourself. When you use the pronoun "you" it shows that you are putting the blame on the other person. If communication could be shown by using arrows, arrows would point to the speaker when the speaker uses an "I" message. In contrast, an arrow would point to the other person if you use a "you" statement. "You" statement arrows could be deflected by the recipient and any change of a resolution could end right then and there with just only a few words being spoken.

Conflict Resolution – Who the Problem Belongs to

Many couples are fine and they get along great until it is time to resolve their problems. It is never reasonable to think that both parties are going to see the problem in the exact same way. The conflict isn't the enemy like most people want to believe it is. All normal relationships will have conflicts. If couples avoid conflicts or they argue until they are exhausted, the conflict will turn into a huge monster that will always be lurking in the shadows. It will be ready to pounce at the first chance it gets.

The wonderful part of great communication is each person values and respects the other's opinion and it doesn't really matter just how different they are. They will accept the other person's right to think and feel the way they do, and this begins the start of a wonderful compromise.

Jacob absolutely hates it when Rhianna leaves her beauty products all over the bathroom vanity. He has asked her numerous times to put all her stuff away when she gets through with it. Every time Rhianna tries to explain why she didn't, she forgot, she was in a hurry, she can leave faster if she doesn't take time to put it up, or there isn't room for all her stuff to be put away. She keeps promising every time that she will start being more aware but each day the products remain on the vanity.

Every time Jacob finds her stuff on the counter, he gets madder and madder inside. He gives up on trying changing Rhianna, but each time they have an argument about something, he will always bring up how inconsiderate she is when she leaves her products on the bathroom counter because she knows it bothers him.

The big question is who actually owns the problem? Some people might say that it is Rhianna's because she won't put her things away. If Jacob didn't care that she left her things on the counter, they wouldn't have a problem, would they?

Has there ever been a part of your life where you have always gotten everything you expected, wanted, or needed? No. Many people think that this is possible in a marriage. It's better to accept the fact that you might get what you want most of the time, and the rest needs to be negotiated. You have to develop ways to negotiate and learn ways to compromise.

When couples go to therapy, the very first thing that each person will say is it is the other person's fault. It makes perfect sense that if the husband states a problem that he is actually the one with the problem. The therapist knows this, but they have to teach it to their clients. If he asked Jacob, he would say that the problem belongs to Rhianna. Rhianna might agree with Jacob if she is codependent.

If you don't know where or with whom to begin, how can you ever resolve a conflict? It would be like trying to start a football game, but no one knows who is kicking off. Once you have it figured out, it will then be possible to get the ball down the field. Jacob kicks off with the problem about the bathroom counter.

Own Your Feelings

Learning how to communicate in ways that will encourage people to take responsibility for their feelings is one way to begin resolving conflicts. If you were to look at Jacob and Rhianna's therapy session, it begins with Jacob saying he has a problem. He has taken responsibility for that problem and how he feels about it. He will then use "I" messages to tell Rhianna his feelings. Once Rhianna has correctly received the message, Jacob will give Rhianna three options for ways she can help him resolve the problem. Rhianna will then agree to one, two, or all of the options. She could also decide not to agree at all.

During this session, it will get rid of any large obstacles that happen when couples try to fix their own conflicts. Their therapist will ask them to give them an actual conflict, so they can begin slowly but they will soon feel what a successful resolution feels like. These tools will work on complicated conflicts and they will work every time. With time, this will be effortless for Rhianna and Jacob and it will melt all the animosity that has grown from years of frustration. Conflicts happen when you are in a relationship, so learning ways to move through them constantly and smoothly will enforce new behaviors. Every couple needs to be invested in communicating well with each other because there will be immediate payoffs for both parties.

Here is an example:

Therapist: "Jacob, you have a problem with the bathroom counter; would you like to start with an "I" message?"

Jacob turns toward Rhianna and this some help from their therapist: "I feel hurt and dismissed when you leave your beauty products on the bathroom counter because I am a bit of a neat freak and it causes my anxiety to take over when I have to deal with that clutter every morning."

Therapist: "Rhianna, don't explain or defend you. Just repeat back what you heard Jacob say."

Rhianna turns toward Jacob and with the help of their therapist: "You feel hurt when I leave my beauty products on the bathroom counter because it makes you feel anxious."

Therapist: "Jacob, is this correct?"

Jacob: "Pretty much, I feel dismissed, too, like I don't matter or I'm unimportant. I guess I also want Rhianna to acknowledge that I did admit that I'm a bit obsessive."

Therapist: "Rhianna?"

Rhianna looks at Jacob: "You feel hurt and you feel unimportant when I leave all my beauty products on the bathroom counter. I noticed you said you were a bit of a neat freak. I do appreciate that."

Therapist: "Did she get the message, Jacob?"

Jacob: "Yes."

Therapist: "Now, Jacob since this problem belongs to you, would you like to ask Rhianna for some help?"

Jacob smiles: "Yes."

Therapist: "I've told you that couples aren't obligated to give each other anything correct? If you would like to have a healthy relationship, both of you need to be willing to give to the other. If you don't, you aren't going to feel loved."

Three Choices

Therapist: Jacob, you are responsible for solving your problems, but let's say that you have a partner who loves you and would like to help you with it. I would like you to ask Rhianna if she might think about giving you, as a fit, any of these three requests that you will now make. Please make your request in this form: A, would you be willing to (state your first request); B, would you be willing to (give your second request); and C, would you be willing to (state your third request)."

Jacob: "I don't need to ask for three things. I just want her to put her beauty products away."

Therapist: "Well, Rhianna might agree to do that and that might be one of your requests. It will help push you away from your one-dimensional position and move you toward a compromise if you would be willing to think outside the box here and find other options."

Jacob smiles and turns toward Rhianna: "Okay, Rhianna, would you be willing to put your things away?"

Therapist: "Great, that is request A. Now, what is request B?"

Jacob: "B, would you be will to use the other bathroom on days that I have early meetings?"

Therapist: "Now, C?"

Jacob: "C, would you be willing to... (He turns toward the therapist) I can't think of anything else."

Therapist: "Take some time to think outside the box."

Jacob pauses and thinks about it: "Okay, I think I have one. C, there is that large drawer on the front of the bathroom counter where we keep odds and ends for the bathroom. If we empty that drawer, would you be willing to open the drawer and sweep all your beauty products into it when you are finished in the bathroom?"

Therapist: "Great. Rhianna, would you please repeat the requests back to Jacob, so he can make sure you heard his requests accurately. What was request A?"

Rhianna: "A, will I put my things away after I'm done with it; B, will I use the other bathroom when he has early meetings; C, we clean out the big drawer under the counter and I just sweep my things into it when I'm finished with them."

Therapist: "Jacob, did she get them right?"

Jacob: "Pretty much, I guess it isn't reasonable to expect her to use the other bathroom."

Therapist: "You can ask for whatever you think will help. It is up to Rhianna to either agree or not to agree. Now, Rhianna, you have the right to agree to one, two, or all of the requests or you can choose to not agree with any of them. What do you think you want to do?"

Rhianna: "To be honest, I don't want to move my things to the other bathroom. That was my least favorite request. I absolutely won't do B. I thought I could do A, but I have agreed to do that in the past but haven't been able to do it yet. If we could empty out that drawer, I could just do one sweep to put all my things away. I won't have to take the time to place everything back exactly where it goes. I can do that. I could do C. (Rhianna turns toward Jacob) Are you sure you are willing to move all the stuff in that drawer? Where would we put it?"

Therapist: "Jacob was the one who suggested it, Rhianna. Why are you trying to talk him out of it when you have just reached an agreement? This might be your codependency surfacing. You aren't used to telling Jacob no. Do you feel guilty?"

Rhianna shrugs her shoulders: "Probably, I don't want him to go to any trouble. I will do C."

Therapist: "Jacob, is there anything you would like to say to Grace?"

Jacob: "Not really."

Therapist: "She did just give you a gift."

Jacob: "Fine. Thanks."

Therapist: "Very good, both of you. We have just used a cognitive behavioral technique to resolve Jacob's problem with the bathroom counter. You both have used new communication tools, which probably seem hard right now. With practice, you will start incorporating them into how you talk and eventually it will just be second nature."

Rhianna: "Do we have to remember all of this?"

Therapist: "That would be a lot to do at one time. No, I am going to give you a handout that you can take with you. It will help you practice using "I" messages and this resolution exercise every day for 30 minutes. It will get easier with some time."

Therapist: "We have started at the behavioral level and I consider this problem solved. In summary, Frank, you have agreed to clean everything out of the top drawer in the bathroom counter. Will you be able to do this today?"

Jacob: "Yes."

Therapist: "That's great. Rhianna, starting in the morning, you have agreed to sweep your products into that drawer before you leave the bathroom. Is this correct?"

Rhianna: "Yes."

Therapist: "Each time you have a conflict, I'd like you to summarize the agreement just like I have done. Your goal is to be totally clear with each other. Tomorrow you have your first opportunity to put this plan to the test. We will talk about how it went in our next session. Good job, you two."

Processing the Resolution

This looks great on paper since it's a behavioral intervention. Assertiveness training, empathy training, and communication training are all formulas that focus on behavior.

If you were to make a recording of the voices during a couple's therapy session, it might show that Line A shows about 80 percent activity where Line B will only show about 20 percent. This shows us another problem with communication and it is one that has been happening for a very long time. One partner talks too much while the other doesn't talk much at all. Line A talks more and gets frustrated. Line B stops listening and gets frustrated.

When a therapist begins with new couples, they will ask them to identify their problems. Communication is the first on the list. If a couple can't talk to each other, they will never be able to solve any problems they have in their relationship. The most important role the therapist needs to figure out all their dysfunctional layers. It is very rare if couples know how to talk to each other when they begin therapy. Communication training is the first thing that the therapist will do. If they try to prioritize therapy in other ways, it would be like pushing the couple into water that is full of sharks.

Once the couple can manage their conflicts, the new skills will become an umbrella that all other problems can be put under. Is therapy really that simple? Nope. Couple's therapy is very complex. If it was easy, everyone would have it figured out. People seek out therapy because they have things that need to be fixed and they don't know how. One more role of the therapist is that of a teacher.

Power Struggle

Many couples make the mistake of getting in a battle with one another when problems come up. Each contestant steps on a platform where they will try to defend their truth. From their positions, every opponent will try every weapon they have in their arsenal to try and defeat their enemy, knock them off their platform while remaining steadfast in their own truth. The person who is left standing will be right and will be the winner of the battle.

Weapons that Are Used in Order to Be Right

- "This is crazy, silly, mean, or ridiculous. You are upset about that?"

This weapon is called the "what is the matter with you." You turn their concern back at them and while discounting all possibilities that their opponent could have true problems because they are flawed. This causes them to be wrong.

- "That isn't what I felt, did, or said and that isn't what you said or did."

This weapon is called rewriting history. It is used to prove what their opponent remembers is false. They won't know what truly happened and they will always be wrong.

- "How can you say that?"

This gets accompanied by tears or anger. This weapon is called the "shut up I can't handle this." You attack your opponent for some negative fault or for being insensitive. You emphasize they are wrong for trying to resolve the problem. Their main goal is to make them feel bad, so they go away.

- "This is totally unfair. I would never get upset about something like this."

This weapon is called the "shame on you or the self-righteous." It is meant to stop their opponent by saying they are crazy for having any concerns. They are wrong for even feeling how you feel.

- "That totally pisses me off."

This is called the "shut up or I will show you what anger truly is" weapon. It gets used to a person's opponent's concerns back on them. It will deflate and divert their concerns by blaming them and these discounts their rights to have concerns. This means they are wrong.

Did you see yourself in any of these arguments? Most people will be able to identify with some of them since everybody wants to be correct and it will become a battle too often.

These examples are typical of a person who is codependent and doesn't think about their loved ones being concerned about them, they remain the center of their universe and they don't want to listen. It is impossible for them not to feel attacked over each little thing that might cause them to defend themselves. Remember that a codependent person doesn't have their own identity. They only have the identity of what they see in their mirror or what their significant other thinks about them. The only hope they have is to change how their partner thinks and feels about them, tire them out, attack them, overpower them, punish them, or prove them wrong until they finally just give up.

Look back over the battle weapons and think about the skills you have been exposed to that might change how you use these weapons against your significant other. These skills might be: being responsible for being unsatisfied, using "I" messages, and the three options skill. You have to take time to think about how you can use them to prevent a battle.

Affirmation

This skill sets a tone for compromise and resolution. If your significant other states a concern, the first thing you have to do is affirm. Most people will get defensive automatically. You have to affirm in a way that is nondefensively that you actually heard their concerns. You can do this by repeating what your significant other has said in your own words. Partner: "Why haven't you finished the laundry?" You: "You thought I would have the laundry done by now?" From this point, the tone has been established. "I have heard from you, now let's talk about it." You have let the wind out of their angry sails and are showing you are a person who will listen to their concerns and move on.

Affirmation isn't what you use at the beginning of the discussion. You use it all the way through to get information from your partner and let them know you are there and you want to help fix the problem. Here is an example:

Partner: "You were home all day, why didn't you get all the flowers planted?"

You: "You wanted it finished today before it started raining tomorrow."

The first time you use this skill with your significant other, they might look at you like you've gone totally crazy. Many people will just wait for you to get defensive before they even get to say their complaint. Most of the time, they are already planning what they are going to say after you get angry and defensive.

Validation

Affirmation and validation are interchangeable. Each one can create a spirit of cooperation and many times they are used together. Validation could be used to accept how your partner feels. If you add validation after affirmation, it could sound something like:

You: "You thought I would have the flowers planted by now. I can totally understand why you would feel this way. It is dark now and it's supposed to rain tomorrow."

Even though this is important, if couples could learn to communicate, especially if there is a conflict, they don't use much validation or affirmation.

You need to be aware of how well you are listening. Do you listen totally without beginning to get defensive in your own head? Being internal is the first thing to do. You have to completely focus on what your partner is saying rather than trying to figure out your comeback. If you can't understand what they are saying, get clarification before you get defensive. See if you can spot the problem during the following scenario where there isn't any validation or affirmation:

Ray: "Honey, is something wrong? You seem distant."

Janet: "That is ridiculous. Why would you think that?"

Ray: "I don't know."

Janet: "Why do you always think something is wrong? For God's sake, Ray."

Ray: "I just miss talking to you. You are always doing something else."

Janet: "Like what? What are you talking about?"

Ray: "You were staring out the window."

Janet: "Really? So, arrest me. I'm in a no stare zone."

Ray: "Just forget it. Stare all you want, I'm going upstairs."

You will see a huge difference with the same situation when affirmation and validation are used.

Ray: "Honey, is there something wrong? You seem distant."

Janet: "You think I'm distant?" This is showing affirmation.

Ray: "I noticed you were staring out the window."

Janet: "I guess I was. If I were you, I'd probably think the same thing. (This is showing validation) Nothing is wrong. I'm just enjoying the snow falling and thinking about when my parents used to take us sledding when we were kids."

Ray gives her had a squeeze: "I love watching the snow fall, too. Do you mind if I sit and watch with you?"

Affirmation and validation are going to take practice. Focus on what your partner is saying, totally listen, and acknowledge you have heard them by affirming what they said. "You think I should finish the dishes now." Ask some questions if you have to clarify what you heard. "What is bothering you? Is it the dishes sitting in the sink?" Don't ever rush a response. Validate. You don't have to agree with your significant other. You just have to validate they have the right to feel what they are feeling. "It doesn't matter if they sit there until after we have walked the dog. I understand that clutter bothers you and you seem frustrated. Is this it?"

These simple but effective skills pack some power. When therapists introduce these two couples, they might try to discount them in the beginning, resist following through or even feel awkward.

When talking about codependent relationships, there will be a bunch of stuff happening underneath the level of communication. It will be hard for some people to admit they don't know how to talk to their significant other. When they come in for therapy, they are on guard about their partner's disapproval. It might be very uncomfortable for a person who is codependent to show their weakness during therapy. It might be hard for them to ask for what they really want. The therapist is responsible for walking that fine line between therapist and teacher, between holding someone responsible and reassuring, especially if their client is codependent.

CONCLUSION

Thank for making it through to the end of *Codependent Relationships*, let's hope it was informative and able to provide you with all of the tools you need to achieve your goals whatever they may be.

If you still aren't sure about making this change, sit down and really look at how your life has been trying to "help" the other person. When was the last time that you did something for yourself? This is the most important thing that you can do if you are still questioning things. You've probably not really looked at your life from a perspective other than the other person. Once you do this, you'll start to realize that changes must be made.

Once you are ready to make those changes, sit down and come up with an action plan. Depending on your relationship with the other person, this action plan can vary. This is where it can get tricky or hard, but this is also where you should find somebody that you trust that can help you to get out of the relationship.

Slowly start to extricate yourself from their life. There will be a backlash, but you will know that you are doing the right thing. Nothing worthwhile is easy. Little by little, you will start to see your life improve. The most important thing is to not let you be pulled back into the relationship with the other person. Live for you, and not for them.

Finally, if you found this book useful in any way, a review on Amazon is always appreciated!

CPSIA information can be obtained
at www.ICGtesting.com
Printed in the USA
BVHW040403040821
613543BV00011B/786